YES, I WILL FOLLOW YOU

Ernie L. Arnold

Cover photo © Katherine's Photography/Katherine Arnold

Text Copyright © by Ernie L. Arnold, 2015

All rights reserved. This book or any portion thereof may not be reproduced or used in any manner whatsoever without prior permission from the author, except for the use of brief quotations in a book review.

Unless otherwise indicated Scripture quotations taken from Scripture taken from the New King James Version. Copyright © 1982 by Thomas Nelson, Inc. Used by permission. All rights reserved. Used by permission.

Table of Contents

Introduction

Called from the Crowds to Oneness
The Overall Template – Circles of Relationship

Chapter 1 – And A Large Crowd Followed Him

Spiritual Discipline 1: The Discipline of Bible Reading and Meditation

Chapter 2 – Receiving and Feeding

Spiritual Discipline 2: The Discipline of Prayer

Chapter 3 – Partnering with God

Spiritual Discipline 3: Fasting

Chapter 4 – The Twelve

Spiritual Discipline 4: The Discipline of Solitude

Chapter 5 – The Power of Twelve

Spiritual Discipline 5: The Discipline of Simplicity

Chapter 6 – Intimacy: The Call to Oneness with Jesus

Spiritual Discipline 6: Worship

Epilogue

Appendix A – Tabernacle Prayer

INTRODUCTION
WELCOME TO THE WALK

"And the LORD GOD formed man of the dust of the ground, and breathed into his nostrils the breath of life; and man became a living being." - Genesis 2:7 NKJV

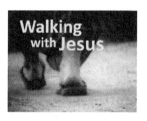

"Now the LORD had said to Abram: 'Get out of your country; from your family and from your father's house. To a land that I will show you. I will make you a great nation; I will bless you and make your name great; and you shall be a blessing. I will bless those who bless you, and I will curse him who curses you; and in you all the families of the earth shall be blessed." - Genesis 12:1-3 NKJV

"The Lord is my Shepherd; I shall not want. He makes me lie down in green pastures; He leads me beside the still waters. He restores my soul; He leads me in the paths of righteousness for His name sake. Yea, though I will walk through the valley of the shadow of death, I will fear no evil; for you are with me; Your rod and Your staff, they comfort me. You prepare a table before me in the presence of my enemies; You anoint my head with oil; My cup runs over; Surely goodness and mercy shall follow me all the days of my life; and I shall dwell in the house of the LORD forever." - Psalm 23 NKJV

"Teach me, O LORD, the way of Your Statues, and I shall keep it to the end. Give me understanding, and I shall keep Your law; Indeed, I

shall observe it with my whole heart. Make me walk in the path of Your commandments, for I delight in it." - Psalms 119:33-35 NKJV

"Then I will sprinkle clean water on you and you shall be clean; I will cleanse you from all your filthiness and from all your idols. I will give you a new heart and put a new spirit within you; I will take the heart of stone out of your flesh and give you a heart of flesh. I will put My spirit within you and cause you to walk in My statues and you will keep My judgments and do them." Ezekiel 36:25-27 NKJV

"Then Mary said, 'Behold the maidservant of the LORD! Let it be to me according to your word.'" Luke 1:38a NKJV

"After these things He went out and saw a tax collector named Levi, sitting at the tax office.

And He said to him, 'Follow Me,' so he left all, rose up, and followed Him." - Luke 5:27-28

"I do not pray for these alone, but also for those who will believe in Me through their word; that they all may be one, as You, Father are in Me, and I in You; that they also may be one in us, that the world may believe that You sent Me. And the glory which You gave Me I have given them, that they may be one just as We are one; I in them, and You in Me; that they may be made perfect in one, and that the world may know that You have sent Me, and have loved them as You have loved Me." - John 17:20-23 NKJV

"But the fruit of the Spirit is love, joy, peace, longsuffering, kindness, goodness, faithfulness, gentleness, self-control. Against there is no such law." - Galatians 5:22-23 NKJV

CALLED FROM THE CROWDS TO ONENESS

Our Walk with the LORD

You have been given a glorious invitation. An invitation that is crystal clear and originates from Heaven above to our Earth here below. You are invited to share in an experience of a life time. You are invited to experience a life of Oneness with Jesus. You are invited to experience what it means to have an Abundant Life, a Spirit filled life, a life of being intimate with the LORD JESUS CHRIST. Will you accept it? Will you step forward and begin the journey towards Oneness?

This little study is dedicated to help you find that direction with passion and purpose. It is dedicated to those who desire a closer relationship and a more intimate walk with the LORD JESUS CHRIST. It is written with the main purpose and desire to be assistance to developing and deepening one's walk with JESUS. It is written to help those who want to walk a Spirit filled life find their own joyous path with Jesus.

For that purpose, that reality of walking intimately with Jesus, that should be our most passionate desire in this life. For we are called not to just initiate that walk with the LORD, but to experience the most intimate and spirit connected life with the LORD as humanly possible. To live out Jesus' invitation of an abundant life (see John 10), one that is fixed on being what authors Robert Crosby and E. E. Speer, along with others have called the life of the ONE. The life of the ONE who has placed Jesus at the hub of their heart, life and soul. That one who has given everything over to Jesus. Not just to emulate Jesus, but to be a vessel overflowing with His Holy Spirit. To be one with Jesus in heart, mind and soul. To be connected, spirit to Spirit.

Is that possible? Yes, for it is that life that we see modeled by saints like Abraham, Noah, Moses, Ruth, Hannah, David, Daniel, Mary, John and Peter? It is that life that we see modeled throughout history in disciples like Augustine, Luther and Susanna Wesley. It was and is the life that has been lived and being lived out in these last days by those like Mother Teresa, Billy Graham, Beth Moore and Richard Foster. Each life unique and distinctive and yet, each life dedicated as others before them passionate about their desire to be as close to the LORD as humanly possible. Individuals who are willing to do all that is necessary to accomplish whatever it takes to be One with Christ. It is this calling of such a life that we see writers like Dallas Willard, Gordon McDonald, Lois Tverberg and Paul Tournier sharing and encouraging us to experience.

It is a life of perpetual progress, a life of dedication, a life of being passionate about knowing God in deeper and deeper ways. A life of becoming ONE WITH JESUS AND THE FATHER AND THE SPIRIT. A life opened for all of us. A life that leads us to the inner circle of relationship with our Savior.

It is not a life void of struggles and its share of ups and downs. In fact, there is no life of absolute perfection (outside of Jesus) here on planet Earth. We all struggle, we all make mistakes and we all choose poorly. However, as John Maxwell says we don't have to allow our failures to define us. We can use our failures as avenues to learn and as pathways that can lead to a life of maturity. Failures do not have to be our pot holes that derail us. They can serve as sign posts that mark a life of progress.

Author Robert Crosby quotes J. Oswald Sanders in his book, <u>THE ONE JESUS LOVES</u>, saying   "We are as close to God as we choose to be." Author and teacher Cynthia Heald puts it this way, "We are as intimate with God as we choose to be." (Becoming a Friend of God, DISCIPLESHIP JOURNAL 54 - page 22). Both are saying the same thing. *"We are as close to God as we choose to be."* At first that little quote may take us aback. Immediately we want to discount its accuracy.   We may even want to put the whole idea up for debate and attempt to present a rational case why that may not be so.   What do you mean we are as close to the LORD as we want to be? Are you saying that it is up to me to determine how intimate, how close I am to the LORD?   But the more we examine that proposition, the more we meditate on the idea, the more we have to come to the reality that it speaks volumes of truth; the more we realize that the LORD has allowed us this freewill choice. We are as close to Him as we have chosen.

The hard fast truth is the reality that you and I are only limited by ourselves. God has made it possible for us to have a deep relationship with Him.   Regardless or our limitations, and in many times in spite of those limitations, God seeks us to walk with us intimately, spirit to Spirit. What we need to acknowledge is the fact that there is no limit to how close we can be to the LORD.

The story of Jacob recorded in Genesis 32 is a prime example of this very fact. For we find him in a wrestling match with the LORD. And it all has to do with their relationship. Jacob has for years followed the LORD from a distance. Wanting to have God's favor and blessing, but not always wanting to be connected with God - our spirit to His Holy Spirit.

One of the pivotal points to the story is when Jacob has to share his name. Now, we know God knew Jacob's name. That was not the issue. The issue was, would Jacob come to a realization of who he was and who God wanted him to become? Would Jacob take a step towards being transformed more into the image of God?

Jacob confesses by sharing not just his name but, his character. Like his name, He had been a "heel grasper". He had been fast and loose with the facts and with people. His whole life up to that point had been one living on the margins. Of staying as close to the moral line as possible but doing his best to make sure that Jacob always came out on top. Whether it was with Esau his brother, or with his father or even his uncle Laban, Jacob did whatever was necessary to take care of Jacob.

In that wrestling match Jacob comes clean. He confesses his humanity and failures. And when we do that, when we come clean before the LORD, the LORD always transforms us. No longer would Jacob be a heel grasper. God would put him on a new path. The path of blessing and continued favor. The path of being a man of God.

While we may question just how well Jacob did in living out that life, the reality is God initiated the path to a life closer to Him. God always does. God is always looking out for ways for all the Jacobs of lives to come before Him and to be transformed into Israels. God has an open ended invitation for a life of connection, of Oneness.

It is my hope in reading this little book and engaging in the exercises that follow each chapter that you will find yourself walking closer to the LORD, connecting your spirit with His Holy Spirit. I hope you will make it your lifelong passion, to be so close to Jesus that, as Lois Tverberg points out in her book, <u>SITTING AT THE FEET OF RABBI JESUS,</u> that you have the dust of Rabbi Jesus always on your clothes. That you find yourself walking down the path of life hand in hand with the HOLY SPIRIT, leading you and guiding you each step of the way.

So, how does all of this happen? How do we walk closer to the LORD? Is there a specific Biblical roadmap? Is there a way to grow closer to the LORD that we all can discover?

Yes, and we are going to share some of those paths in the following pages. We are going to share some of the paths that have been lived out by our brothers and sister of the Bible. They will help point us to the way. But in the end we will learn that we each have our own path with the LORD. He has a pathway that has our name on it. It is one that has been fearfully and wonderfully made and designed for us. It will be very similar to those who have walked before us, but as His Sheep who know His voice, He knows us all by our names. He knows all of us by who we are and He has a walk, a way, a path laid out for us to walk with Him.

Let's join together in this prayer from Psalms 25

"To you, O LORD, I life up my soul. O my God, in you I trust; let me not be put to shame; let not my enemies exult over me. Indeed, none who wait for you shall be put to shame; they shall be ashamed who are wantonly treacherous.   Make me to know your ways, O LORD; teach me your paths. Lead me in your truth and teach me, for you are the God of my salvation; for you I wait all the day long."

THE OVERALL TEMPLATE - CIRCLES OF RELATIONSHIP

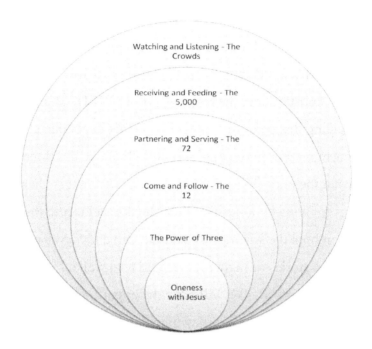

Okay, over the next few pages I want you to know that you are invited to begin, or perhaps retrace, or even start anew your walk of intimacy with the LORD JESUS CHRIST. We each find ourselves at different places on this life long journey. For some who read this little book, all of this will be a refresher. It will be a nice little reminder of continuing your walk. For some, it will hopefully challenge you to move closer to the LORD, to examine where you currently are, and to be a challenge to draw closer to the LORD. For some it may be an eye opener. You may not have been aware that God seeks to draw you closer and closer to Him. And for some, it may even be a starting point. You may have read about Jesus but never realized that He was calling you to connect with Him, spirit to Spirit.

ULTIMATELY, our journey should lead to the "inner circle" or what others have called the intimacy or relationship of the ONE. By "ONE" they have alluded to that relationship that was shared by the likes of the Apostle John, the ONE JESUS LOVED. But, by no means are they saying that John was the only one that experienced that depth of relationship.   For in reading Scripture I believe that John was certainly not the only ONE. Rather, John in writing his Gospel was inviting us to journey alongside him as he drew closer to the LORD. The Bible in both the writings we call the Old and New Testament is filled with the stories of numerous people who walked with the LORD with the same purpose. We will have the opportunity to meet some of them along the way of our journey together. In the end, you and I will hopefully rejoice in being a part of the "ONE".   The "ONE" who has joyfully accepted Jesus' invitation to experience an abundant life, a life of being filled and led by the HOLY SPIRIT. A life of one - our spirit with His Holy Spirit.

Robert Crosby, along with E. E. Speer, have done an excellent job in sharing with us that around Jesus there existed a number of different types of relationships. There existed a number of different levels of the depths of relationships that people had with Jesus.   Both men used the ideas of circles to represent these relationships. Crosby calls them "RINGS OF THE LORD" or "CIRCLES OF CHRIST."

I think they are correct and using part of their material as a template, I would like for us to examine each of these different relationships and the invitation of each to draw closer to the LORD. There are six in number, each existing in one another, but progressively drawing closer to the heart of Jesus.

    CROWDS

    THE 5,000

    THE 70 (some versions will say 72)

    THE TWELVE

    THE THREE

    THE ONE (go back and look at the illustration on page 8)

Each circled relationship has its own particular characteristics and traits. Each circle is unique in and of itself. And while one can stay in one of the outer circles, Jesus invites us to draw ever more closely to Him. The same is true that we can leave one of the inner circles and go back and forth. For they are not to be seen as concrete in nature, but fluid. We find ourselves in certain areas of our walk with Christ, wanting to be watchers and listeners in certain areas where Jesus is calling us to being One with Him.

Through looking at each relationship circle we will experience life stories that further invite us to grow and to mature. For example, we will see Jesus inviting all those that start off in the crowd to come out and join Him in experiencing a deeper relationship. This is part of the stories of the Gospels. In John 17, the writer shares how Jesus prays for us to experience the ultimate relationship, that of being - ONE

WITH HIM. This is Jesus' deepest prayer. This is Jesus' deepest passion and desire. Listen again to His words, "that they may all be one, just as you, Father, are in me, and I in you, that they also may be in us, so that the world may believe that you sent me." (John 17:21).

Enough talking. Turn the page and let's get started.

CHAPTER ONE - AND A LARGE CROWD FOLLOWED HIM

"And as he left there and went to the region of Judea and beyond the Jordan, the crowds gather to him again. And again, as was his custom, he taught them." - Mark 10:1 (ESV)

"That same day Jesus went out of the house and sat beside the sea. And great crowds gather about hi, so that he got into a boat and sat down. And the whole crowd stood on the beach." - Matthew 13:1-2 (ESV)

"After this Jesus went away to the other side of the Sea of Galilee, which is the Sea of Tiberias.

And a large crowd was following him, because they saw the signs that he was doing on the sick." - John 6:1-2 (ESV)

Jesus was simply captivating. It doesn't take long in reading Jesus' story to be aware of that fact. Soon after His baptism and His wilderness trials we see large crowds of people beginning to follow Him. There was something about Jesus, the way He communicated, the way He interacted with people. People were drawn to Him like metal shavings to a magnet.

Luke tells us that Jesus' teaching displayed an authority that was astonishing. (Luke 4:3132). His words possessed an authority that others lacked. Wherever Jesus went there was an air of excitement, of electricity. Wherever Jesus showed up in an area, supernatural things happened. The Gospels are full of reports of all kinds of physical healings, of exorcisms and people finding wholeness and peace for the first time in their lives. We read stories of families being restored and lives made new. Jesus was teacher, healer and miracle worker all in one very attractive and alluring package.

Anyone who has been around a fire knows how it draws people. There is just something appealing and fascinating about fire. People want to see its flames, feel its heat and experience its majesty. Jesus was like fire. He was like a supernatural flame. A flame that compelled people to come and see. And come and see they did, crowds by the hundreds and thousands. All wanting to see and listen to this carpenter turned rabbi.

It is no different with us today. Where there is excitement, where there is heat we are drawn to it. And when we read the words of Jesus, when we take time to hear His voice, we find ourselves among the crowds wanting to see Him, experience Him and be in His Presence. Even 2000 years removed, His words, His teaching, and His presence draws us.

In many ways, our individual stories are parallel to those of Jesus' crowds. We all start off in a very similar place. Pretty much, we all start off on the same emotional and spiritual terrain. *We all begin by being members of a large crowd that seeks to listen and watch Jesus from a safe location.* We want to hear what Jesus says, we want to watch what He does, but we want to do it from the sidelines. We don't usually start our walk with the LORD by starting in the inner circle, but rather it is from the fringes that we begin our journey with the LORD. We start off as crowd followers, watchers and listeners.

The Scriptures reveal to us that we are all born into a crowd. A crowd called for lack of a better term - Fallen Humanity. Romans chapter 1 shares with us some things about this crowd. It's a crowd that includes all of humanity. It is a crowd that includes everyone who has ever been born. It is a crowd that goes by still another name in Scripture called, "THE WORLD". It is because of this crowd that John 3:16 - 17 shares with us that God loved so much that He sent His one and only Son, Jesus, to die for in the first place. It is a crowd that displays all the characteristics of being broken by sin, of living without purpose and meaning. It is a crowd that so many times is even unaware of its own needs, its own sinfulness. (Ephesians 4:17-24). It is a crowd that desperately needs to be rescued. It is a crowd that needs a Savior (Ephesians 2:1-10). It is a crowd that can only be reached by and through the Holy Spirit (John 16:4-11). It is as members of that crowd we initially discover ourselves living, existing. It is a crowd that suffers from deep seated emptiness. An emptiness and a brokenness that comes as a result of SIN, both corporate and personal sin. A moral and spiritual bankruptcy that is of our own making.

For whether we would like to admit it or not, we all have chosen our lives of brokenness. We may attempt to lay the blame on others, but the reality is we all have chosen at some time to rebel, to forsake, to live a life of brokenness (Romans 5:12). We have chosen to take our own bite of the apple and we see its effects all around us. While we may blame Adam for the fall, the reality is that all of us can look back and see our own individual sinfulness. *"For we all have sinned and come short of the glory of the LORD"* (Romans 3:23). We have all sinned.

It doesn't take a great deal of common sense to comprehend this reality. Can we not testify that we see all around us example after example of our world's brokenness? Have we not witnessed enough displays of self-centeredness to testify to this truth? We humans seemingly never tire of trying to find happiness through worldly ambition and power; but, in the end we know that there has to be something more, something better for us in this life. We know deep down that there is something missing. Like the writer of Ecclesiastes, we can see that all of life without God is vanity. That without God, life is simply going from dust to dust. Surely, there must be a higher purpose to our living here on earth. We feel deep in our DNA that we are not here by accident, that we are not some cosmic accident. There must be a plan, there must be meaning to all that is around us. If not, then all of life is just eating and drinking and taking pleasure. And while we may want to adopt that philosophy, there is inside of us a call to a higher life. There is something crying out to us that we can find life, abundant life.

We come to understand through the leadings of the Holy Spirit, through the Word of God that we were put here on earth for a purpose, a reason. We were wonderfully and supernaturally made in the image of our God. We were created just a little below the angels in heaven.

(Psalms 8) God Almighty smiled on each one of us as He breathed His Holy Spirit into us and gave us light and life.

At first we may not fully know or understand the reason for our life, for our personal existence, but we can sense the fact that we have been given one. (Jeremiah 29:11). And so, we feel a call to leave the crowd called the world. We feel a call from somewhere to go and seek for something more. More than just physical life. And so, we leave a part of one crowd to join yet another crowd. A crowd very similar to the ones that followed Jesus. A crowd of curious watchers and followers. A crowd of learners and listeners. A crowd that sought to know more, to understand more and to experience more, than they currently were living.

And somewhere, by someone, through something we were introduced to Jesus. We were introduced to His teaching, His words. We may not even remember when it happened. We may not even remember who it was that introduced us to Jesus for the first time. We just know that at some time we accepted the invitation through the leading of the HOLY SPIRIT and we were brought into the presence of Jesus.

For some of us it happened because we were blessed to be raised in a loving body of Christ's disciples and therefore were introduced to Jesus at an early age. It seems we have always followed Jesus. The path was made easy for us. We were surrounded by those that loved Jesus and us. They saturated us with prayer as they waited for us to receive and accept our own call to begin the journey with Jesus as

Savior and Lord. They rejoiced with us and became our spiritual mentors and continued to pray and assist us on our walk. We became fellow travelers in the footsteps of Jesus.

For others, it may have been when we first picked up a Bible and started to flip through it. Out of curiosity we wanted to know what was in it. Did it really contain the words of life? Who is this one called Jesus in the first place? Can He really rescue us? Can He really live within us? Can He really give my life meaning and purpose? What we did not know at that time was that the Holy Spirit was patiently leading us towards Jesus. We did not pick up that Bible by accident. It was part of God's divine plan to bring us home to Him.

Our journey could have started right after we heard someone talk about their life being transformed for the better. How that once life had no meaning and now it was full of purpose and direction. As we listened, they told us all this was because of Jesus. Jesus had made their lives have meaning. It was Jesus that gave life purpose and direction. It was Jesus that reached down and picked them up out of a life of sin and brokenness. It was Jesus that brought them new life. And suddenly, we too wanted to know more about this one called Jesus.

However it was for you or even how it is becoming for you, the reality is that you and I started hearing and responding to the invitation of God's Holy Spirit. We did not start this journey alone. All along God has been whispering to us, leading us, guiding us to a life of relationship with Him. He has been inviting us along to leave behind the larger crowd of humanity, of the world and started walking with the crowd that begins to listen and watch Jesus.

And while even now some of us may not be ready to join the Jesus group yet; that's okay. God is patient. He allows us to just first come and see, watch and listen. At least that is what He did for me, even at a young age. He gave me time to understand, to process and to know what and who I needed in my life.

I had been going to church all my life. I can't think of a time that my family did not attend church. We were a three time a week family - Sunday morning, Sunday evening and Wednesday night services. When Revival meetings came, we were there every service, day and night. Church was a normal part of our everyday existence.

My home church was approximately a tenth of a mile from our home, so come rain, snow, ice or sleet we usually made it there on foot. Each week you would have seen my mom, my three siblings, and myself all walking to church. Only a severe illness resulted in our absence. And by severe I mean high fever, confined to your bed illness.

My mom had not always been a church goer, in fact she had not always been a believer. She had experienced some great tragedies in her earlier life as a result of her sins. She found herself basically on the wrong side of the tracks, broken and lonely. Someone told her about Jesus. Someone invited her to church. Through JESUS her life was transformed. She was drawn to Him. She desired to live for him as passionately and as sold out as she had been sold out to sin.

She wanted her children to experience a life of holiness. She wanted us not to avoid making the same mistakes she had made in her earlier life. She wanted us to experience a better life. And to her, the best way for that to happen was to make sure every time there was church, her and her children would be in attendance. Nothing was going to stop her from saturating us with prayer and the message of Jesus Christ.

Attending church and being a part of the Body of Christ are two very different things. One can attend church faithfully for years and still not be a part of the Body of Christ. It wasn't until I personally received Jesus as My Savior, as I invited the LORD in my heart, to forgive me of my sins did I become a part of the Body of Christ, the Kingdom of God here on earth.

Even as a child there was a hunger to know more about Jesus. There was something about Him that was absolutely appealing. For me, it was as natural as eating and breathing. I now know that I was being lead by the Holy Spirit. As a child I was open and receptive to His calling. It was all a part of God's plan. I know now that all we have to do is listen and follow. God initiates evangelism. All He needs is harvest workers (Matthew 9:35-38).

And so, I started reading as best I could. At a young age, I read all the stories from the Bible. Mom made sure that I had a Bible and always encouraged me to read it. While we worked around the house she would turn on the radio so we could hear Christian music and preaching. She filled our day with prayer, Bible reading, and Christian radio.

I listened to others at the church and I looked at their lives. Were they happy? Did they find joy? Was Jesus real in their lives? Did they really love Jesus? Did I want what they professed, what they possessed? Thankfully, I had a great upbringing and a great church family. All around me every Sunday were people who loved Jesus and loved one another. I did experience their joy, their peace and love. They all gave Jesus credit for their lives.

Then one day it happened. My brother and I were helping around the church raking leaves. Mom thought it was good for us not only to go to church, but to get active in church. And since we were old enough to rake our own leaves that meant that we were old enough to rake the leaves at the church. So, after asking the pastor if we could help and he agreeing, we walked to church rakes in hand, ready to get to work.

What I did not know was that my mom wanted the pastor to have some alone time with my brother and me. Our dad was not a believer, so we did not have any kind of positive male spiritual influence. So, mom created a space for us to be around our pastor. He would be able to help us and in turn we could help the church. She was a wise woman.

While we were raking, our pastor patiently spent time explaining to us who Jesus was and what He could do in our lives. We would rake a little and then we would rest a little. He explained to my brother and me that Jesus was more than just a GET OUT HELL Savior. He was God. And as God, He wanted to be a part of our lives. God loved us more than anything. He told us how God had created us and that He had a purpose for our lives. He then told us that if we would allow Him, God would show us how to live. God would make our lives better. And that one day we could go home with Jesus to live with Him forever and ever. But it was up to us.

Basically, he told each one of we could stay a part of the crowd and just watch and listen, or we could take a step forward and become a part of Jesus' disciples. We could step out from the crowd and join the Jesus crowd. I really don't know how many leaves we raked that day, but I do remember asking Jesus in my heart and life that day. I do remember that day was a very special day; it was the day I began following Jesus. Thank God for mothers who pray and make a way for their children to know and accept Jesus. Thank God for a loving church that made it so easy to see Jesus in others. Thank God for reaching down and rescuing a whole family.

That day I accepted Jesus' invitation. It would be the first of many invitations to follow Jesus. It would be the first of many times that Jesus called me to come closer to Him.

You may be where I once was - just a part of the crowd, an interested part, but all the same just a part of the crowd. For many years perhaps that is what we do - watch and we listen. We just stay in the crowd.

Exodus 19-20 talks about such a crowd. It seems like God has always had this great crowd of watchers and listeners. People who want to be near God, but not yet ready to be a part of God. As usual, God always invites them to come closer, to come out of the large crowd and follow Him and experience a deeper walk with Him. That was certainly true of the Exodus crowd in chapters 19-20.

They had been a crowd that had both seen and heard a great deal from the LORD. They had listened to His servant Moses and watched God do incredible miracles on their behalf. They had experienced firsthand God's rescuing grace. Firsthand they had experienced God's call out of slavery and into His fellowship of peace. They had watched God rescue them from the clutches of Pharaoh and the enslavement of Egypt. With their own eyes they had watched the sea divide and in their own sandals they had walked across dry land. They were a free people. Free to live their own lives. Free to live a life of righteousness.

And now came this whole new opportunity, God was inviting them to an even deeper walk. God was inviting them to come out of the large crowd of humanity and take a deeper step with Him, to not just be free physically, but to be free spiritually.

At first it seems as if they were ready. Exodus 19 tells us that they made careful preparations. They were consecrate themselves, they were wash their garments and restrain from any sexual contact. In other words, they were to do all they could to purify their hearts, minds and souls. But as Exodus 20:18ff shares with us at a crucial moment the people of God, took a step back. They choose to not be in direct communion with the LORD. They choose not to hear His voice. They decided while they were appreciative of the physical freedom He gave them they were not ready for the intimacy of being with Him.

And yet, in Exodus 20, God still desires to speak to them. God Almighty wants to have an audience with them. In no way, was God interested in destroying them but in bringing them deeper into a walk with Him. But as we read in verse 18-21, the people decided to stay in the crowd. They were not ready for such intimacy. They simply could not understand that God was on their side even after all that He had done for them. They allowed the devil to exaggerate their fear and in fear they kept away.

Instead, they decided to let Moses be close to the LORD. They would allow Moses to be their mediator. He would stand in their place before the LORD. They would relinquish their intimacy with the LORD through Moses, a mere human being. What the LORD offered them was a relationship that they chose not be to ready for at that time. They would instead just depend on human Moses. They allowed their fear and their guilt to keep them away from the LORD. They missed the opportunity to receive so many blessings and anointings. They grieved the Holy Spirit that day and so God had no other choice but to allow them to continue to follow Him at a distance. God invites, but God will not force Himself on us. We choose how close we want to be with the LORD. Sadly, they choose poorly.

But the same cannot be said of a little man in the Gospel of Luke named Zacchaeus. When he was given a very similar opportunity to come close to the LORD, he took full advantage. What Zacchaeus lacked in physical stature he did not lack in spiritual passion and zeal. He capitalized on his opportunity to leave the crowd and become a vital part of the Kingdom of God. He had enough of life being normal, He wanted an abundant life.

As we read his story (Luke 19:1-10), Zacchaeus starts off being just a member of a large crowd. A large crowd that was following Jesus, watching and listening. Listening and watching. Being moved by Jesus words but not knowing if they wanted to move with Jesus. A crowd that if they liked Jesus' words might follow him the next day. But also a crowd that if they dislike what Jesus had to say would leave him in the dust. For that is the way it is with crowds. While they are large in number, the truth is crowds are diminutive in commitment. For anyone who has been a part of a crowd or has had the eye and ear of a crowd well knows that while you may have their eyes and ears it is quite another thing to have their hearts.

That is the danger of continually staying with the crowd. While crowds provide a certain measure of safety and anonymity, they can also be quite fickle. They can sing praises one day only to cry out for crucifixion another. The Bible tells us that the same crowds that decided to ascend up the Sermon on the Mount and can also live in the Valley of the Golden Calf. Great numbers, potentially wonderful, but also more often than not, low commitment with many always having one foot out the door.

While we see Zacchaeus starting off in the crowd we don't see him remaining with the crowd. Jesus looking inside his heart and offers Zacchaeus an invitation for a life of intimacy. A life of following Jesus. Zacchaeus is granted an invitation to be with Jesus. Does he stay just a face in the crowd or does he accept the offer of Jesus and enter into a deeper relationship?

That is what my pastor shared with me many years ago. The opportunity to know Jesus more than just a man in some stories. He told me that Jesus wanted to do more than be a story to read. That Jesus wanted to come into my heart and live. That Jesus wanted to bring salvation into my life. That is the same invitation that Jesus gave Zacchaeus. It is the same invitation that He reaches out and shares with all of us.

We all start off in the crowd. Walking, listening, watching, and pondering. The question that we have to answer is a rather simple one - Will we stay in the crowd or will we step out and respond to Jesus' invitation of following Him? Will we allow Him to come to our home (our hearts) and bring salvation?

Zacchaeus accepted Jesus invitation and his life was forever changed. I love the way Luke 19:10 puts it - "TODAY SALVATION HAS COME TO THIS HOUSE". Today, salvation (soteria), deliverance, safety, redemption has come to your house. (Luke 19:1-10).

At first, all Zacchaeus wanted was to watch and listen. He first just wanted to find the best place to see and hear what Jesus was saying. That is usually our starting point as well. In the end, Zacchaeus was invited to experience salvation, deliverance and redemption. We are invited to experience all of this as well.

My pastor prayed for me that day. My life changed. I allowed Jesus to come into my heart, my life that day. And the journey that started that day has continued to this day. Even as a young child I came away from the crowd and into the inner circle of discipleship with Jesus.

If you have not made that choice you can. The same Jesus that invited Zacchaeus to be a part of his life is the same Jesus that invites all of us. Perhaps, you have been in the crowd, just watching and listening and now it is time for you to take the next step towards Jesus.

Join me in this simple prayer:

Dear Lord Jesus,

I do believe that You are who You say You are - the very Son of God. I believe that You died on the cross for all my sins and that today You are here to grant me forgiveness and salvation. Please come into my life, forgive me of my sin, and make me a member of Your family. Bring salvation to my life, my home, my heart. I want You to be the very center of my life. Thank-you for Your gift of eternal life and for Your Holy Spirit, who now lives within me. You are the way, the truth and the life and in You I commit myself. I pray in the strong name of Jesus today. AMEN.

If you have prayed that prayer or one like it, you have stepped out from the large crowd and now are following Jesus. In the next chapter we shall see what it means to begin to follow Jesus. To go from the "large multitudes" that followed Jesus to being a part of those that literally took days out of their lives to follow Him. For lack of a better term, we will call them the 5,000.

Below is an invitation to begin to practice one of the time honored Spiritual disciplines called Bible reading/meditation. You will find one of the spiritual disciplines at the end of each chapter. It is our hope that you find your walk with the LORD deepened as you practice each discipline.

SPIRITUAL DISCIPLINE # 1 *
THE DISCIPLINE OF BIBLE READING/MEDIATATION

The goal of reading the Bible and meditating on it is to enable us to hear God more clearly, hearing God more clearly enables us to better live a life of holiness, of living out an Abundant Life. Hearing Him enables us to be drawn into the relationship of the "ONE".

While some other forms of meditation have a more personal inward goal, Christian Spiritual Meditation is dedicated to listening, sensing and obeying the life and light of Jesus Christ. And this discipline is usually best accomplished as you open up God's Word and engage in its richness and beauty. There is simply no better way to engage your spirit with God's Spirit as He reveals Himself in and through His Holy Word.

Is there a perfect way we can read the Bible? Perhaps not, but are there methods and practices that we can utilize to help us better identify with God's Word. There are methods that we can employ to receive more out of our times of reading Scripture.

Bible reading/meditation is of its own nature a more passive discipline. It is characterized more by the art of reflecting and pondering than upon direct didactic study. It involves more listening, more waiting, more stillness than active thinking. When we meditate on God's Word we are not as much trying to grab as we are attempting to open ourselves up to receive what is already present. We are inviting the Holy Spirit to reveal Himself to us through His Word. We are waiting for God to whisper in our hearts, our minds, and in our spiritual ears. When in fact, God is always ready to whisper into our lives. He actively seeks relationship. God loves to communicate with His children. However, at times we suffer from poor hearing and busy schedules. We read, but we don't always take the time to meditate. We don't always take the time to "chew" on God's Word.

But there are ways to correct this behavior. There are ways for us to be more open to hearing what the LORD wants to say to us through His Word. To do this there are some general steps we are encouraged to begin taking each time we sit down and read the WORD.

Step 1: Simply begin by becoming quiet before the LORD.

Invite the Holy Spirit to come and bring you into a place of stillness and tranquility. Think of this time as you and the LORD sitting down by the still waters. Begin by breathing slowly and allowing the Holy Spirit to calm your heart, your mind and your soul. Prepare yourself for a wonderful adventure with the LORD.

For some of you this may trigger a time of great anxiety because you have too many things to do and you have trouble being still. The mere mention of being still causes every atom in your being to start moving around. You would rather do almost anything than having to be still. Just thinking about it causes anxiety.

Don't fight those emotions. Release them to the LORD. He made you. You are His creation. He understands your heart, your anxieties. He understands you better than you do yourself. If suddenly as you are trying to get quiet all kinds of ideas come rushing in your mind, simply try this - have a small pad of paper with a pen and when suddenly a thought of something comes to mind, jot it down. Don't allow it to enslave you. Put it to the side. You can get to those things later.

We must refuse to allow this quiet time to be stolen from us. *Ask the Holy Spirit to guard your heart and your mind.* We need to "be sober-minded; be watchful. Your adversary the devil prowls around like a roaring lion, seeking someone to devour." (1 Peter 5:7-8). The Devil loves it when he can destroy our quiet time with the LORD, so don't allow him to do it. Make up your mind to call on the name of Jesus and get quiet in the presence of the LORD. The Bible tells us that we can cast all our anxieties on our LORD, because He cares for each of us. Don't fight this battle alone. Your Shepherd will lead to still waters but you must follow Him.

Step Two: Now, read a portion of Scripture slowly. Read it out loud, hear the Word.

The Bible is not just to be read, it is to be heard. It is to be absorbed into us. Allow it to sink into the depths of your being. Be like the Prophet Ezekiel, take it and eat of its wonder and joy.

Allow it to become a part of your life. Don't see it as mere words, but as words of light and life.   *Don't attempt to read too much at one time*. Always remember you are not in a race. You can't read all the Bible in one sitting anyway so why try?   Your goal is to hear from the LORD, not to impress Him with all the words you have read. What you are trying to do right now is provide an opportunity for God to reveal His Word to you at this point in your walk with the LORD. This is Your Daily Bread Time. Don't rush it and don't allow it to spoil.

Think of it like you would a wonderful breakfast meal. You have all the ingredients before you, eggs, milk gravy, grits, biscuits, jelly, bacon, and sausage. It's the feast of a lifetime. Don't just dig in, devour, and then run and get the antacids. Instead, enjoy your feast. Smell the bacon, look at the beauty of the eggs, savor the taste of fresh buttered biscuits.   Allow it to be more than just a meal. Allow it to be an experience. The same is true with God's Word.

Breathe the passage in. If you have another version of the Bible, read the same passage from that version as well.   Remember, unless you read Hebrew, Aramaic or Greek what you have before you is only a translation. While some may feel a kindred spirit towards one translation, the reality is they all attempt to translate God's Word as accurately as possible. Every translation has merits and shortcomings, but all are able to reveal to us God's Word.   Find a version that speaks to you, the one that you can understand the best. It will not be the same one for everyone. Even as you grow, you may be lead to another translation.   Remember, the goal is to allow the Holy Spirit to speak to you through His Word, and that is done best if you first of all can understand that Word.

Personally, I am drawn to the New King James Version. I was raised with the old King James and the New King James seems to be a great substitute. It seems to have the cadence and the rhythm in reading that I am most familiar. At the same time, I have enjoyed greatly the NIV, RSV, NASB, and the ESV which I have used a great deal in citing passages. I have also very much enjoyed the MESSAGE and the LIVING BIBLE and the work that went into writing them. However, it must be pointed out that they are paraphrase editions of God's Word rather than a direct translation. Now exactly, what does that mean?

("A paraphrase is a retelling of something in your own words. A paraphrase of the Bible is therefore different from a translation in that a translation attempts (to varying degrees) to communicate as "word-for-word" or as "thought-for-thought" as possible. A paraphrase takes the meaning of a verse or passage of Scripture and attempts to express the meaning in "plain language". Using a source like, THE MESSAGE or the LIVING BIBLE should never be our primary Biblical source. Rather, their goal is to act more as a commentary than on an actual reading of God's Word. They serve as great helps but in reading God's Word we are best advised to use a translation.")

Step Three: Take some time to now chew, to meditate.

Let's take a moment and look at the story of the 5,000 recorded in John chapter six, verses 1 through 15. Read it slowly. If you have a parallel version take time to read it.

Take a moment to think about all that is going on in those verses. All that the writer wants us to capture as we read the words he wrote. For now, just concentrate on those 15 verses. Later on, it would be good to review this passage in its larger context, looking how this passage fits into the whole theme and scope of John writing His Gospel. But for this exercise, simply contain yourself to those fifteen verses.

Imagine first of all of being in the crowd that followed Jesus. Put yourself in that crowd of watchers and listeners. See yourself among the crowd. All around you are all kinds of people, young and old, rich and poor. All of you have been listening to Jesus teach most of the day.   All of you have been glued to His every word. None of you want to miss anything He says or does.

Especially what He does. For you have watched with utter amazement as the blind have had their sight restored. You have watched and been amazed at how many crippled people are not for the first time able to walk upright and without any pain. All kinds of various diseases have been healed all around you.   You rejoiced and celebrated along with others as their lives have suddenly been transformed. Your heart has been sadden with seeing so many people in so much pain, but then your heart has soared as you have seen miracle after miracle, healing after healing. It has been almost too much to take in at one time. Just how many have been healed, and who is this Jesus?

The air is electric with excitement. God's Spirit is moving everywhere. Jesus is teaching with an authority that has not been heard since the time of Moses. You know that you are a part of something supernatural and you are basking in the overflow. You find yourself overwhelmed and need a time to process, but you can't leave, you are afraid you will miss something. Something supernatural, something spectacular. Something you have never seen or even thought possible.

However, you notice a rumbling in the pit of your stomach. You are getting hungry, and you are not the only one. All of you have followed Jesus, listening as He walked and talked and now you and a whole lot of others are miles out of town. Miles away from the shops and bread stores and you are hungry. Your stomach just growled. Other stomachs around you are growling as well. You look around and everyone seems to have the same look, they too are getting hungry.

You know back home that there is plenty of food. Your family made some fresh bread just this morning. But you are not back home. In fact, you are quite a distance from home. All of you had planned to spend most of the day with Jesus and so you had all brought a little food to tie you over. But with all the healings and the teachings time slipped away and now you and great many others find yourselves late in the day, miles from home with no food in sight.

You do the only thing you can think of, you ask around for some food, for some bread. And sure enough, you discover that others are in the same shape. They too had brought a lunch or a snack thinking that they would be home by dinner time. But everyone just got caught up in all the miracles and the teaching and now all around you people were hungry as well.

Even Jesus notices it. Perhaps he is beginning to hear the stomachs of all those around him, rumbling and growling. Perhaps even the Incarnate Son of God Himself is suffering from a few hunger pains. But what could be done? Where in the world could you get enough bread to feed this lot? And who in the world would bring it much less be able pay for it. This is starting to not be a nice situation. People are starting to get anxious and a little grumpy. Suddenly, all the good will that you have experienced has begun to evaporate away. Suddenly, where once your felt the safety of the crowd, it is beginning to transition into anxiety and uneasiness.

The disciples also notice what is going on and you watch as they go and talk with Jesus. Perhaps it is time to call it a day. They know that all of the good will that had occurred through the healings and teachings would soon disappear once everyone started getting hungry and grumbling. People would start voicing their unhappiness. No one likes a hungry crowd, especially if they can't get find any food. Pretty soon the disciples knew this crowd was going to turn on them much like a similar crowd years before turned on the Prophet Moses and Aaron (see Exodus 16). The disciples knew that the same crowd that had been happy and full of joy could also begin to pick up rocks and sticks and a riot could ensue. A complete disaster was in the making.

All of a sudden, you see little boy running up to Jesus. One of Jesus' disciples was leading him as best he could, but the little boy was more agile and was able to get though the crowd quicker. He had something in his hand to give to Jesus. Like a great many children he had gotten so caught up in all the listening, running and playing so much that he hadn't eaten his lunch. He still wasn't hungry and he overheard Philip looking for food. It could have been that this boy himself had been touched by Jesus. Perhaps he had been lame or crippled and had received a healing touch from Jesus. Now, if that were the case then we don't have to wonder why he had not eaten.

You can imagine his joy with being able to run and play freely for the first time. Food, no doubt, was the furthest thing from his mind. Who wants to eat when you can run and play and have a great time with your friends? While we don't know for sure if this is what really happened, we can live in the moment with this possibility. We can allow ourselves to imagine this happening. This is a part of allowing the Scripture to come alive in our minds and hearts.

We do know this, the little boy steps forward and gives Jesus his meal. Maybe he only wanted Jesus to have it. After all it was only a small lunch, just a few pieces of bread and some small fish. He knew it couldn't feed everyone, but Jesus had to be hungry and more than likely the boy just wanted to share his meal with Jesus. After all, Jesus was the most important person on the hillside that day. You look over the scene and you smile.

Now, what if that little boy happened to be your little boy? What if that boy happened to be you? How would you react? What would you do or say?

Step Four: Reflect, Ask, Seek and Knock

A person could spend the rest of the day in just this little story. But just for a few moments allow the Holy Spirit to lead you through some questions as you reflect.

1.   Try to put yourself in Philip's place or one of the other disciples - how do you find enough bread? What caused you to go and look for bread in the first place? What kind of heart does it take to notice the hunger pains of others? What does this tell us about the disciples?

2.   Try to put yourself in the little boy's place. Why hadn't you eaten your meal already? What caused you to go the whole day without eating? What caused you to speak up when you overheard Philip looking for food? What made this little boy willing to surrender all he had to Jesus? What lessons does he teach us about giving and surrendering? What example does he show us about allowing Jesus to have what is already in our hands?

3.   Try to put yourself in one of the parent's places who suddenly is anxiety ridden over your children crying out for food. What do you

do now? Will suddenly all the wonderful feelings and emotions of the day be swept away with the pains of hunger? How many times does our physical wants get in the way of us experiencing a time of spiritual growth? How important is it that our children's physical and spiritual needs are met in Sunday School, Children's Church or small group?

4.   What comes to your mind when suddenly you see the disciples passing out all the bread and fish and you know that moments before they had none? Where did they get the bread? What is going on? How do you understand it? Even if you attempt to rationalize it as the bread coming from other's leftovers (like the boy's lunch) you know that there is too much bread and fish for that to be the only answer. You are left with only one answer - God has provided this meal through Jesus. What does that mean?

5.   Perhaps what runs through your mind is suddenly this Jesus not only can heal the body, but feed the body as well. Just who is this man?   How do you process it all - the healings, the teaching and now this miracle?

6.   How do you go out today and receive from the LORD   the healing that you need, the teaching that your desire or the miracle you need to meet a need that seems impossible? What does all of this say about Jesus love? What does all of this say about Jesus meeting needs? How can you be Philip - working with Jesus to find food for others? How can you be the little boy who surrenders all that he has so that the needs of others are met? How can you today allow God to use what He has already given you?

In just a few moments you begin to understand that this story is one that you can quickly read and begin to meditate on. It is one of those stories with more than enough cud to chew on. In reading it, you see that God is sharing the reality that He is able to meet all your needs and others needs as well. But you also understand that in meeting those needs, He is looking for those that will share from their resources. He is looking for people like the little boy who will surrender what they have so that it may meet the needs of others.

Step Five: Internalize it - Make it personal: Allow it to speak to you.

Now, that you have read, that you have allowed the story to come alive - take a moment and allow Jesus to meet your need. Simply share with Jesus what is in your heart - your needs, your fears, your hopes, your desires. Simply pour out your heart to the One who can meet all needs. He is here. He will meet your needs today.

But don't stop there for you are invited to go a step further. You are invited to take your hands, your mind, and your resources and offer them to the LORD. By doing so, you step into the same sacred space as Philip and the little boy. You are invited to surrender what you have to be used by the LORD to meet the needs of others. And those others include your family, your friends, and others all over God's world.

Now, as you begin to pray, you ask the LORD to help you this day to both enjoy and rejoice in the "daily bread and fish" that God will provide for you this day. You ask the LORD to show you how you can partner with Him to provide "bread and fish" for others that also are in need. You become Jesus for others.

What you have just done is more than just read the Scripture. You have done more than just allow yourself to read a string of words to mark off your Bible reading for the day. You have taken the time to breathe them in your life. You have feasted on some of their riches. You have allowed the LORD to speak to you. And you are ready to take that Word into the rest of your day.

Now, finish this time of feasting by taking a moment to thank the LORD. Don't just leave His presence without consecrating your time with thanksgiving and praise. Rejoice in your spirit.
Praise His Holy Name! Praise Him for His Holy Word.

Write down something that He has spoken to you. Commit to pray for ways you can live out this passage. Seek a way today to be a means of grace to someone else. Find someone today who needs "your lunch" to help meet their needs. Share with someone who is in need that the answers they seek can be found in an intimate relationship with Jesus. We all live busy lives. Or at least we say that we do. But where do those busy lives really get us? For all our running around, what do we really receive? Most of the time if we really think about it we spend a great deal of time running around in circles and at the end of the day all we have to show is tired minds and muscles. We can all agree with Ecclesiastes - *"A generation goes, and a generation comes, but the earth remains forever. The sun rises, and the sun goes down, and hastens to the place where it rises. The wind blows to the south and goes around to the north; around and around goes the wind, and on its circuits the wind returns. All streams run to the sea, but the sea is not full; to the places where the streams flow, there they flow again. All things are full of weariness; a man cannot utter it; they eye is not satisfied with seeing, nor the ear filled with hearing. What has been is what will be, and what has been done is what will be done, and there is nothing new under the sun."* - Ecclesiastes 1:4-9.

You and I were made to dwell on God's Word. For it brings us comfort, strength and is one of the most excellent ways that God speaks to us. His Word reveals to us our paths to walk. His Word calms our fears and gives us strength for the day.

In closing, understand that at times meditation may not always be an easy spiritual discipline. But it will happen the closer you draw to the LORD. Thomas Merton reminds us of this fact in sharing with us these words:

"If you desire intimate union with God, you must be willing to pay the price for it. The price is small enough. In fact, it is not even a price at all; it only seems to be with us. We find it difficult to give up our desire for things that can never satisfy us in order to purchase the One Good in Whom is all our joy - and in Whom, moreover, we get back everything else that we have renounced besides!

The fact remains that contemplation will not be given to those who wilfully (sict) remain at a distance from God, who confine their interior life to a few routine exercises of piety and a few external acts *of worship and service performed as a matter of duty. Such people are careful to avoid sin. They respect God as a Master. But their heart does not belong to Him. They are not really interested in Him, except in order to insure themselves against losing heaven and going to hell. In actual practice, their minds and hearts are taken up with their own ambitions and troubles and comforts and pleasures and all their worldly interests and anxieties and fear. God is only invited to enter this charmed circle to smooth out difficulties and to dispense rewards." (Thomas Merton, WHAT IS CONTEMPLATION? - in <u>SPIRITUAL CLASSICS</u> edited by Richard Foster and Emilie Griffin, page 18-19).*

The Psalmist prays: *"Give me understanding, that I may keep your law and observe it with my whole heart. Lead me in the path of your commandments, for I delight in it. Incline my heart to your testimonies, and not to selfish gain! Turn my eyes from looking at worthless things, and give me life in your ways."* (Psalms 119:34 - 37).

Today, take some time and become still before the LORD. Your life will never be the same. Your walk with the LORD will never be the same. And now that you are primed to walk deeper with the LORD, let's go together and join a deeper walk, the walk of the 5,000. Turn the page and let's continue our adventure into intimacy with the LORD JESUS CHRIST.

CHAPTER TWO - RECEIVING AND FEEDING

"And they all ate and were satisfied. And what was left over was picked up, twelve baskets of broken pieces." - Luke 9:17 (ESV)

"When they found him on the other side of the sea, they said to him, 'Rabbi, when did you come here?' Jesus answered them, 'Truly, truly, I say to you, you are seeking me, not because you saw sings, but because you ate your fill of the loaves. Do not labor for the food that perishes, but for the food that endures to eternal life, which the Son of Man will give to you. For on him, God the Father has set his seal." - John 6:25-27 (ESV)

"Jesus said to them, "I am the bread of life; whoever comes to me shall not hunger, and whoever believes in me shall never thirst." - John 6:38 (ESV)

And they all ate and were satisfied. That sounds nice doesn't it? You can easily imagine the scene. All over the hill side there were adults and children sitting and laying down on the lush green grass, finishing off the last of their fish and bread sandwiches, wiping their faces with just the ends of the corners of their robes. They were smiling and filling good, taking some time to just rest, time to let the food settle for a few minutes before getting back on the road walking toward home. Instead of everyone grumbling with growling stomachs, now they would go well feed and well rested.

What a day it had been for everyone. Jesus' amazing ability to teach, His use of word, of all those sick people coming to Him to be healed. All the miracles they had witnessed among the crowds. Lives had been radically and supernaturally transformed before their very eyes. And how about that food, boy, did hit the spot. What a way to end the day. Just who was this Jesus, this man, this one that people were calling Prophet? I mean, wow! WOW! Who would have thought there would be more than just his teaching and the miracles? But to end it with food from heaven. That's more than they could process. So, let's just lay down a moment, enjoy the time, and then we will walk back home. Boy, do we have a story to share with our families and friends.

There is nothing better than having a great meal and filling full and satisfied, being able to take a time out and just rest after a big meal. Knowing that everything is well in our world. What a day it had been for all of them. A day that had surpassed anything they had ever experienced. A day that they would be able to share with their children and grandchildren. A day they not only saw miracles, but they, themselves became a part of a miracle story. Oh, as they rubbed their full stomachs - life sure is good. This Jesus can meet any need. We need Him around a lot more often. They could enjoy a day like today more often than not. If only Jesus would stay around and teach some more, heal some more, and of course, pass out some more of that bread and fish.

The only problem with our good times is they are permanent. Our good times do not last forever and ever. That full filling we experience when life is going well, all too often doesn't last long; at least as long as we want them. In no time we find ourselves yet again hungry. Yet again, we are in need of someone to meet our requests, wants and desires.

Our hunger doesn't cease. In fact, it often intensifies. Once one of our need areas is taken care of we begin to want other areas of our lives to experience fulfillment. We want our relational, emotional and even our spiritual parts to find their individual foods and experience fulfillment. We want to experience a "holistic fullness." We desire someone or something to meet all of our every growing needs and desires.

And like the crowds, we too look and long for a Savior, one who will meet all of our needs. We like being a "receiver and feeder" lined up in front of Jesus. We like coming to where Jesus can meet all of our needs, where Jesus can meet all of the needs of our family. This is one of the most appealing things about Jesus to most people. We love those times when we know that we have been filled. We love Jesus' fish and bread moments.

Being a citizen of the 21st century we are well aware of our neediness. Millions all over the globe are searching each day to find a purpose for their finite existence. They do their best to answer big life questions. Why have they been born? What are they to do with this life they have been given? What can they do to give their lives significance? After all, life has to be more than just power and possessions. Aren't we entitled to enjoy life? Shouldn't there be someone who can not only provide us with all the answers, but also be able to deliver them? After all, we did not choose to be born. So, aren't we entitled to some "receive and feed"?

I mean look around our world. From the largest of our cities to the most rural areas of our nation, we find all manner of angst. Our society is riddled with generational abuse, parental abuse, parental absence, violence, poverty, marital discord, overwhelming grief, loneliness, and mental anguish. The list could go on and on. We try to deny all of these hoping that the band aids of more money, more government or more education will cure our ills.

But it is just not true. If anything, life has shown us to be the truth, it is that neither money, the government, nor even having a job, can bring us the happiness we so desperately desire. We are a broken people. We find ourselves a broken people, living in a broken world, full of broken hopes and promises. Our world needs a Savior.

Dr. Tim Clinton in his book, <u>Caring for People God's Way</u> succinctly points out our current brokenness:

35% of people who get married will end that marriage with a divorce or lifetime separation.
18% of those who choose divorce will eventually get remarried only to divorce again.

75% of all children living in a fatherless home will at some point in their childhood experience severe poverty.

By age 18, 33% of all girls and over 17% of all boys will be a victim of sexual abuse. Most abuse will come by someone they love or should be able to trust.

Annually, over 5.3 million acts of domestic violence are reported to the police.

All of this speaks volumes about out brokenness. Our need for a Savior. And there is more.

According to the 2008 National Survey on Drug Use and Health, in the US there were 8.3 million adults who had serious thoughts of committing suicide. Of that 8.3 million, some 2.3 actually made plans to commit suicide, with 1.1million actually attempting suicide. Over 33,000 succeeded in taking their own lives. More recent data has that number climbing to 41,149 with over 836,000 Emergency Department visits. (http://www.cdc.gov/nchs/fastats/suicide.htm).

Twenty percent of those living in the United States will face and have to deal with a measured time of depression. Many will be placed on some type of medication (four of the most common are Cymbalta, Lexapro, Zoloft, and Prozac) that they will take for the rest of their lives. Depression is the disease of our modern age.

Nineteen million adults will suffer from maladaptive anxiety, giving themselves over to irrational fear, panic, and dread. They too, will be given medications, many never to find permanent relief. They will suffer from this crippling anxiety the rest of their lives.

Had enough? We haven't even alluded to such issues like financial setbacks, workplace demands, overall loss, unplanned pregnancies, cancer, obesity and the many other physical issues affecting our society today. Alongside of being called the digital age, our time has also been called "THE ASPIRN AGE". However, we can all attest to the fact that it seems like all our societal headaches never go away. They simply have become immune to our societal drugs and therapies.

So, is it any wonder that once we understand that Jesus is the Answer, we don't rush to Him for all our answers? We are so overwhelmed with the pains and brokenness of our age that we have no other choice. And is it wrong? After all who can solve all of the issues of our lives? Who else has all the answers? Who better than Jesus to cure our ills? Who better than Jesus to take care of all our needs?

The truth is, we find ourselves very much like those that made up the 5,000. Like them, we are smart enough to realize that we have "no bread and no fish," but we know that there is one called Jesus that can meet every need. So, all we need to do is follow Jesus. All we need to do is to hold out our hands and receive all His healings, favor, and blessings. All we need to do is to "receive and feed." Answer found. Need supplied. Case closed.

Jesus will meet our needs. He will take all that we have to give Him. We can lay all our anxieties, all our burdens and all our pain on Jesus. He will take it, remold it. Bless it, and make our lives wonderful.

But Jesus desires more than just being our problem solver, our way to a free lunch. Our Lord is simply not interested in becoming a Supernatural Wal-Mart where all our needs are met at the lowest possible price. Jesus desires more than this type of relationship. He wants to be more than our bread maker and our filet of fish server.

Turn to John 6:13-15 and you will see what I mean. *"So they gathered them up and filled twelve baskets with fragments from the five barley loaves left by those who had eaten. When the people saw the sign that he had done, they said, 'This is indeed the Prophet who is to come into the world! Perceiving then that they were about to come and take him by force to make him king, Jesus withdrew again to the mountain by himself." (ESV).*

The crowds that were gathered that day, understood the power of Jesus. So, they decided that they would take it upon themselves, to make Jesus their king. After all, He could meet each and every one of their needs. The easiest thing, therefore to do, was to give Jesus a throne, to proclaim Him to be their king.

However, Jesus doesn't need for you and me to make Him King. He doesn't need us to cast some heavenly ballot to vote him into kingship. Revelations 19:16 tells us that Jesus is already the King of King and Lord of Lords. He doesn't need for us to cast Him a crown or build Him a throne. He is God. Always has been, always will be. Amen.

Jesus did come to earth at that time to set up an earthly kingdom. While that was certainly within His power, it was not His utmost desire. What Jesus sought for both them and for you and me is for us to desire a relationship that is deeper than just a 5,000 food and chips type relationship. A relationship that is only out for the free bread and the fish.

Jesus wanted them to step up their game. Out of love and compassion Jesus had met all their needs. He had taught them, healed them, and feed them. But it was all done to bring them into a closer, deeper relationship. A relationship of where they would become His partners. A relationship in which the focus would not be on them just "receiving and feeding," but where they would rest in Him. Where He would be their Bread of Life.

Most of us were first drawn to Jesus because we thought He could meet our needs. We saw Him meeting the needs of others and we wanted to see if He could meet our needs. We came to realize that we needed Jesus and so we accepted him as our Savior.

Things started off well, our hearts, our minds and our lives were changed. Our needs were met and life was good. But then one day it happens, because it always happens. One day the manna (the supernatural blessings) so to speak, begin to occur less frequently and in fact, they may disappear altogether. Our daily milk is no longer being delivered to our spiritual doorstep.

There is no more free fish and chips. Wal-Mart Jesus is no longer greeting us the door, doing all He can to meet all of our wants and wishes.

We find ourselves having this relationship with Jesus, but we start feeling like we got the short end of the stick. What gives? What happened? We liked this Jesus; this Jesus that comes down and meets all our needs. This Jesus that gives me goose bumps and makes me feel good all inside. This Jesus that becomes the fix of all my ills, the cure for all that bothers me.

Did He disappear? Was it all a gimmick? Had we been sold a bill of goods? Was none of it real? Did we get spiritually scammed? Was it just a bunch of spiritual pallor tricks? Is this just another spiritual Ponzi trick? Now what?

And so, we go to find Jesus only to have Him start saying the craziest of things. We open God's Word and read such passages as John 6:53-58 and Matthew 16:24. We read things that lead us to once again wonder who Jesus really is and what does He really want? We read things that make us stop and wonder about everything that has do to with God, Jesus and the Holy Spirit.

I mean, what is all this Bread of Life stuff. What is Jesus trying to say? And what does Jesus mean by this command to follow Him means that we are to deny oneself? We came to Jesus to have our personal needs met. We came for the teaching, for the healings and yes, for the bread and fish. We are not sure that we want to sign up for

"I am the Bread of Life" speech or the "Deny Yourself and Take Up Your Cross" drive.

It is right here that we find ourselves at the same crossroads as the Crowd of 5,000. They wanted their needs met, but they were not sure about growing deeper in Jesus. The Bible tells us that in that crowd of 5,000 many left never to be seen or heard from again. *"After this many of his disciples turned back and no longer walked with him."* (John 6:66 ESV) Notice, these were not just crowd watchers and listeners; but, disciples - those that had decided to follow Him. Many had already taken that first step to follow Jesus, but not really know Jesus.

For Jesus calls us to a deeper walk. A walk that will not always be easy. A walk that will test our minds and our souls. A walk that will require sacrifice and surrender. A walk that will involve the death to our ambitions, our amusements and our agendas. A walk that will leads us to die out to sin, to self and become alive in Him and through Him.

Following Jesus requires faith, and that is not a human ability we can just muster up. Faith is a gift from the LORD (Romans 12:3) and every one of us has been given a certain measure of faith. The key is, will we put it into practice? Will we allow our faith to grow, to enlarge and become more and more real in our lives. A few disciples that day continued to follow Jesus; many, many others choose not to follow Him any longer. They just walked away.

Jesus could have had thousands fall at His feet. He could have allowed them to build Him an earthly kingdom. It was all for His asking. After all, who wouldn't want to follow the One that could take care of all your physical needs? Who doesn't want to follow the Great Physician, the Miracle Worker, or the Bread Maker? Who doesn't want to follow the One who fills the nets with fish over flowing?

But, who wants to sign up for believing that Jesus is the Only Way? Who wants to commit their heart and lives believing that Jesus is the True Bread of Life who provides all that we shall ever need? Who will surrender themselves to a life in which we need no one else but Jesus? Who wants to follow the One that takes up a cross and asks us to take up one as well? That is precisely the life, the experience that Jesus is calling us.

Jesus is calling us to a deeper relationship that the one that was experienced by the 5,000. He is calling us to live a life in which we believe that Jesus is more than a Bread Maker. He is calling us to experience Him as the BREAD OF OUR LIVES (John 6:35). It means that we connect with those like the disciple Peter in proclaiming that in Jesus is there everlasting life. It means we experience Jesus more than Teacher, Prophet, Healer, and Miracle Worker. We experience Jesus as LORD, SAVIOR, LIFE, GOD.

To take a piece of bread from Jesus is one thing. For Jesus to be the Bread of Your Life means something all together different. In the former, Jesus is a mere messenger. He is a mere servant who gives us a piece of daily nourishment. He brings the Bread but is not the source of the Bread. In the latter, we begin to understand that Jesus is the source of True Life. It is only in Jesus we find Life, Everlasting

Life. It is only in Jesus we find Truth. It is only in Jesus we find true salvation, redemption and purpose.

The Apostle John shares with us the story of one that chose to follow Jesus in that very manner, of making Him Lord of her life. She willingly commits all of herself to Jesus! Not immediately, but the longer she and Jesus shared sacred space, the more she began to understand and the more open and receptive she was to Jesus' invitation. We find her story in John chapter four, the Woman at the Well.

The Woman at the Well is a multi-facet, multi-relational woman. As you read her story, you notice something interesting. You can chart her spiritual walk growing deeper with Jesus the longer she talks with Him. She begins by simply watching and listening. In no time, she begins to understand that through Jesus her needs can be met. But then, she begins to understand that Jesus can more than just meet her physical needs, He can be that which gives her life meaning. She travels through the land of "receiving and feeding" to the new ground of partnering and serving. All of this is done in just the few hours that they share together. That is important for us to understand.

All of these relationship circles over lap and intertwine with one another. They are dynamic and vibrant. While it does take time to travel deeper with the LORD, the amount of that time is fluid and not static. One is not limited to one's relationship with the LORD. If we desire, we can grow deeper in the LORD in mere minutes where other people may take years. The more one gives of themselves to the LORD, the deeper the relationship. This is exactly what we see happening in the spiritual walk of the Woman at the Well. Once she realizes who Jesus is, she quickly accepts Him whole heartedly and grows by leaps and bounds in a matter of minutes. For what seems impossible with man is possible with the LORD.

John's initial portrait of her is of a person that was not even a part of the "watchers and seeker" crowd. His first portrait is that of a complete outsider, a person that has no desire to be a part of anything. Not only is she broken she also has a pretty big chip on her shoulder. In fact, it's not really a chip, it's more like a log or a big bolder sitting up there on her shoulder.

If you would have been able to talk to her, she would have quickly told you that she had a right to have that boulder. She had a right to have an attitude. Her life had been anything but trouble-free. Her life was a mess and she had the scars to prove it.

At one time I am sure she had considered herself privileged and perhaps even a woman highly favored. No doubt she had at one time lived a fine life, but that was five husbands ago. All five of her spouses had either died, turned her away or a combination of the two. Currently, the man she was co-habituating with either did not respect her or was oppose to marriage. I don't think this was the life she wanted to live. At that time she may have had little choice. It was very common for a woman in her condition to be forced to live in less than ideal condition just to survive. All one has to do is to read some of the stories of what happened to many of the women in the American West around the turn of the 19th century to find women in similar conditions. Women who had lost a husband or been put out only to have to result to working in a saloon to survive. What we do know is that in talking to her Jesus speaks truth to her, but does not look down upon her or treat her as a person without worth. He does the exact opposite, He treats her with respect and He invites her to experience a life of "oneness" with Him.

It is interesting how Jesus approaches this woman. At first, Jesus meets posing as the person who is in great need. He asks her for a drink of water. He no way of getting any water out of the well, she does, so He asks her for some water. He puts himself under her control. She can either provide him some water or she can refuse. It's all up to her. At first Jesus took her completely by surprise. His kind (Jewish) didn't mix with her kind (Samaritan). Over the past 400 years there was little love lost between the two ethnic groups. One held on to the oldest of traditions while the other claimed pureblood status. Each believed that the other existed only so that Hell would be populated. The most water either side ever shared with each other was from the spit they sent in their direction.

Yet, here is Jesus asking her for water. Here is Jesus reaching out to her, showing her that he needed her help. You can imagine her shock. Here was this man, this Jewish man speaking to her a woman, a Samaritan woman at that. Who in the world does he think he is, and what in the world is going on. No doubt, she had her guard up. She had been the victim of too many men who had used her and thrown her away. She might talk to him, but she was going to keep her guard up.

In the end we know as we read the story, it would be He who gives her water, Living Water. And while many of the 5,000 rejected (John 6:60 - 67) the depth of relationship that Jesus so desired (that of being the Bread of Life - the Source of Life), the Woman at the Well and her village readily accepted. They accepted Jesus as Messiah and as Living Water. They accepted and believed that Jesus was indeed the Savior of the world (John 4:42).

One story takes place at a well, the other on a hillside. However, both deal with the same central issue. Are we ready to truly follow Jesus? Are we ready to see Jesus more than just a man who can meet our physical and emotional needs? Are we ready to accept Jesus as that One in whom we find True Life? Are we ready to see Jesus as the Savior of the World?

Are we ready to follow Him past the cups of water, pass the loaves of bread, past the plate of fish to allow Him into the most inner parts of our lives? For that is what it means to take in living water, to take part of the Bread of Life. It means that we believe that Jesus is more than just another human being. It means that we belief that Jesus is the Source of Life. That Jesus is Life. It means that just as water and bread give us life physically, Jesus is able to give us life emotionally, relationally and spiritually and physically.

Jesus wasn't wanting us to somehow become spiritual or physical cannibals or vampires - eating His flesh or drinking His blood. That was the mistake the group back in John 6 made. They allowed the devil to cloud their thinking. They misunderstood what Jesus was offering them. Jesus was desiring them to experience Him as Savior and LORD. To experience His life giving us life.

Jesus wanted them choose to live above the natural. He wanted them to see Him, experience Him. He wanted to pour His Spirit into their Spirits. They were seeking a bread that would be here today and gone tomorrow. He was offering Himself, Lord of Lords and King of Kings.

Earlier in Jesus' encounter with the Woman at the Well, He had revealed to her that true worship only happens when our spirit connects with God's Holy Spirit. Jesus told her that God is Spirit, and a person's deepest connection to God therefore must therefore, occur in spirit. A person's spirit is the highest part of their being. The spirit is that part which lasts when the physical part has gone back the way of the earth. It is our spirit, therefore which is the source of our highest dreams, thoughts, desires and hopes. Jesus was offering to all who would follow Him, this supernatural connect between us and God, the connection of Spirit to spirit. Jesus was offering to all the highest of all worship, "oneness" with the Father, Son and Holy Spirit. All they had to do was to connect their spirit with His Spirit. All they had to do was to be cleansed, sanctified and justified by the power of God.

It should not have been difficult to understand. Jesus was offering them, and He offers us, true humanity. We all know that we have life because of the fact God breaths into all of us life. That is what the Genesis account of creation teaches all of us. "*Then the LORD GOD formed the man of dust from the ground and breathed into his nostrils the breath of life, and the man became a living creature."* (Genesis 2:7 ESV) About every five seconds we experience that reality. We breathe in and out about 10 - 15 times a minute. It is something that we do quite naturally. We don't have to think about it.

And along with that human breath we take in, Jesus invites us to breath in His Spirit. He invites us to allow Him to control our breathing, our lives. Jesus desires to be our sustenance. He desires to be more than just one who can meet our temporal needs, He wants to meet our everlasting needs as well.

Jesus knows that we have a deep hunger. A hunger that cannot be satisfied with earthly food. We are more than just eyes, and ears, and a nose and a mouth. We are more than hands and feet and arms and legs. We are in essence spirit. We are made to exist outside of time. We are supernatural. We are God breathed. We are more than temporal. And deep down we know it. Deep down there is something inside of us that agrees with Psalms 8:4-5 - *"what is man that you are mindful of him, and the son of man that you care for him? Yet, you have made him a little lower than the heavenly beings and crowned him with glory and honor."* (ESV)

We look outside at the vastness of the universe and know that we were made to experience all of it. We look inside the depths of the microscope and know that we were made to understand and experience that world as well. Our bodies groan because they know they cannot forever be the shell that houses this spiritual temple of ours. We know we are more than what we see, but the devil does all he can to convince us otherwise. And all too often, many believe his lies. They believe his lies and accept as truth that this life is the only life. And so they do their best to just live lives in this shell. They buy, they sell, they do their best to accumulate and build their own little kingdoms denying the fact that in a few short years the only thing they will be occupying is 84X23X24 inch box at best or a 200 cubic inch urn. A life given by God but used up in wasted living.

God wants more for us than this kind of living. Jesus shares that in Him we can forever have that breath, that light, that life. That in Him there will be no end. But we decide to step out from the 5,000 and go beyond a fish and chip life. We must step out in faith by grace alone and accept the living water of Jesus.

That is what the Woman at the Well did. That is what the little boy who surrendered everything in the hands of Jesus did. Others have done as well. Peter did this after much struggle. So did James and John. And so shall we if we make the same choice. We can choose Jesus. We can make Him our Savior.

It is our choice. God gives us this right. However, it is one not to be taken or made lightly. For to choose life in Jesus requires us to follow Jesus. And in following Jesus we know that ultimately there is a cross (Matthew 16:24). And no cross is easy to pick up. Much less carry. For all crosses lead to the same place. The place of a death. A death of sin, of selfishness, of self. A death of thinking that the world revolve around you. A death of only seeing yourself and your needs. A death of our own ambitions, agendas and amusements. A death of always coming to the table of Jesus seeking what is there for you. We die out to Jesus. The ending of St. Francis' prayer for peace tells us the truth -

*"It is in giving that we
receive; it is in
pardoning that we are
pardoned; and it is in
dying that we are born
to eternal life"*

Many are called few are chosen. Few choose to accept true life. For who wants to choose death. But it is only through death that we can experience true life. It is only through surrender our lives to Him that we suddenly are able to see things to wonderful to imagine and explain.

And so like the Woman at the Well and the little boy we can choose to walk away from the 5,000 to enter into a deeper circle of relationship with Jesus. Others around us may leave Him but something inside of us knows that only He has the real answers. Only He can give us real life. Only in Jesus can we experience what it means to be truly human.

And so we look around and there it is - it's our cross. It is waiting for us to pick it up. Ultimately we know we don't die for ourselves, we cannot, but we do die to ourselves. We do not have the ability to become our own Savior. It's beyond our capacity as fallen humans.

Robert Crosby correctly states that the biggest barrier to leaving the large crowd and following the 5,000 is unbelief. Unbelief allows for a time to listen and watch but in the end causes us to never step out of the crowd. Selfishness causes us to hesitate in going deeper with the LORD. Selfishness causes us to not go deeper than the 5,000. If we want to experience "oneness" with Jesus we must die. Let us pray together.

Dear God,

I thank You for meeting all my needs. And now God, You call me to follow You closer and deeper. You call me to pick up a cross and really depend on You as my living water, my bread, my breath, my life. You call me to deny myself so that You may open up a whole new walk with you.

I am tempted to walk away. I tempted to go back into the crowd and attempt to disappear again among the crowd. To attempt to just meet my own needs. To substitute real living water and bread for the riches of this world. I am tempted to just want you for your gifts. I am tempted to just want to follow you just so all my needs are met. I tempted to want you like a fix for an addiction. But in the end I sense a deeper need. A need to acknowledge You as Lord of my life. A need to give over to you total control and receive a deeper healing. A healing that goes beyond anything I have yet experienced. A healing of my soul, my inner spirit, my mind and my heart. A healing that I know will open up new doors of discipleship. And it is into those doors that I want to walk through. Only You Jesus have eternal life. All others are imitations. But You are real. And so, by faith and in faith I give

You all. I surrender all to You. I open up all my mind, my heart and my soul to be filled with Your Holy Spirit.

Thank you Jesus for inviting me down a new path. A path of more than just needing and receiving. Thank-you for leading me down a path in which I rest solely in You. AMEN.

This chapter reveals to us that it is quite a journey going from the crowds to the 5,000. We have seen how this the next step involves hearing and processing some hard sayings of Jesus. It means accepting Jesus as more than just our Miracle Maker, our Bread warmer and our Cup Holder. It means allowing Jesus to be the Miracle in our lives. And it means Jesus is inviting us to allow Him to be the substance of our spirit and true life to our soul.

However, we are just beginning our walk of adventure with Him. For as wonderful as it is to be a part of the "receiving and feeding" crowd, He invites us to a whole new level of relationship. A level of partnership; where we are allowed not just to "receive and give" we are invited to work alongside of Jesus as His partner. This is the level that we examine in the next chapter called the CALL TO PARTNERSHIP. But before we get there let's take part in another Spiritual Discipline. This one involves the discipline of prayer.

SPIRITUAL DISCIPLINE # 2
THE DISCIPLINE OF PRAYER

"True, whole prayer is nothing but love." - Saint Augustine

"Give me a pure heart - that I may see Thee,
A humble heart - that I may hear Thee,
A heart of love - that I may serve Thee,
A heart of faith - that I may abide in Thee." - Dag Hammarskjold.

"Now Jesus was praying in a certain place, and when he finished, one of his disciples said to him, 'Lord, teach us to pray...'" - Luke 11:18 (ESV)

There is nothing as wonderful, as deep, as mysterious and mystical as prayer. It is something that is so easy to do and yet one of the most difficult spiritual disciplines to put into daily practice. As Richard Fosters shares with us, "Prayer ushers us into the Holy of Holies, where we bow before the deepest mysteries of the faith, and one fears to touch the Ark."

We need not be shy when it comes to prayer, for God invites us to come into His presence to share freely. We are drawn to prayer, to communicate with God and yet there is something that causes us to be repelled, to hide from prayer. Who are we to come before the Almighty? Who are we to talk to the LORD?

And yet, the Bible shares with us that this is God's deepest desire, to communicate with us in our prayer times. For prayer is more than a ritual of human monologue. Prayer is the language between lovers. It is the language of love shared between our Savior and ourselves.

Somewhere, somehow we got this mistaken idea that in order to truly pray we have to have the right words. We have to do it the right way. We have to know and use the right formula to truly pray. Prayer is therefore like some form of math problem or scientific formula. If we can get the right "form" then we can pray and rejoice in answered prayers. After all is that not what we want most? Answered prayer? God answering our prayers. God doing what we want Him to do for us and our families?

To see prayer in that fashion is to see prayer much like the 5,000 saw the loaves and fishes. Prayer takes on the form of a shopping or gift list. We have a list of things we want from God and prayer is the way that we get them. Prayer is the key for us to get all that we desire. After all, did not Jesus say to Ask, Seek and Knock. Didn't Jesus, Himself tell us that we could ask anything in His name and it would be ours?

True Prayer is deeper than a shopping list or us asking for things. Our God is not some kind of Super Amazon.com or Supernatural Wal-Mart. He has promised to meet all of our needs. That is a given. True prayer involves relationship. True prayer involves companionship. True prayer is time spent in fellowship. True prayer is when our spirits share sacred space and time with God's Spirit.

True, earnest prayer involves transformational change. True prayer is God's way of providing a pathway for us to be taken over by His love and joy and peace and patience and kindness and goodness and faithfulness and gentleness and self-control. True prayer is communion with God and when we experience communion with the LORD then transformational change is evident.

The LORD wants to share our prayers. Even our prayers that are full of our wants, our concerns, even those that are laced with our pride, our vanity and conceit along with our egocentricity. For in our prayers we open up ourselves, our real selves without any worry of being rejected or destroyed. The longer we spend with the LORD in prayer the more we are formed into the image of Jesus.

Scripture is full of all kinds of prayers. Prayers that start with people exactly where they are at that time. Scripture shares with us some lofty prayers like the prayer of the Virgin Mary who only asks to be a handmaiden for the LORD. Other prayers are more earthly like Jonah complaining about God's mercy and grace given shown to his enemies. Jonah wanting God to not hear the prayers of repentant Ninevites. Jonah had to learn about God's compassion and it was through prayer that this lesson was given.

Moses spends some time in prayer complaining and wondering what to do about his congregation while Daniel becomes an interceding warrior of prayer for God's exiled people. Elisha brings judgment upon those who mock God, while Paul prays for those that have wounded him deeply. Isaiah confesses his unworthiness while the Psalmist rejoices in his walk of righteousness. All of these prayers were heard and all they answered. But with each season of prayer the relationship between them and the LORD drew closer. With each prayer they were transformed in the image of the LORD.

As we approach prayer there are some things that we can do to assist our prayer time.

1. **Just begin where you are.**

Very simply, just begin where you are with the LORD. Pour out your heart to Him. Just believe that God will hear and accept your words. For the truth is this. God can only bless you, listen to you, answer you, lead you, guide you where you are because where you are is the only place you are at this time. For Moses, the encounter with the LORD happened in front of a burning bush. For Abraham it occurred on the back side of the desert. For Noah it was in the midst of a hellish world. For Ruth it was in a time of immense grief and poverty, picking up wheat leftovers. For Esther it was the oncoming threat of Jewish genocide. For us it is here and now. Right now. Wherever you find yourself right now.

Just open your mind, your heart and begin to pour yourself out to the LORD. Just start by talking to the LORD like you would to another person in the room. For even though you may not be able to see or sense His Presence, you can be assured that God is present.

2. **Invite the help of His Holy Spirit.**

The Apostle Paul understood the difficulty in praying at times. At times it is hard for all of us to prayer. God does not want us to pray alone. Again it is not a grocery list or a monologue. Prayer is a partnership. It is a sharing of love between us and our LORD.

So, Paul tells us in Romans 8:26-28 that we are invited to ask for the HOLY SPIRIT to help us. *"Likewise the Spirit helps us in our weakness. For we do not know what to pray for as we ought, but the*

Spirit himself intercedes for us with groanings too deep for words. And he who searches hearts knows what is the mind of the Spirit, because the Spirit intercedes for the saints according to the will of God. And we know that for those who love God all things work together for the good, for those who are called according to his purpose." (ESV)

God is passionate about our spending time with Him. He wants to share sacred space and time. But we don't always know how to do it. So, He provides a way. His Holy Spirit has promised us to help us find the very words to say, to express. The Holy Spirit will search our hearts to find out what our deepest desires are, what our hopes, our plans and what is truly on our hearts and minds. And the Holy Spirit will begin to transform them into thoughts and words that will open up Heaven's door of blessings and anointing. All of us have a supernatural prayer partner - the HOLY SPIRIT.

3. Experience Prayer as a Privilege and not a Duty

Please don't view or regard prayer as one of your Christian duties. Prayer was never a duty with Jesus. Prayer was as natural to Jesus as breathing and as eating. Prayer was Jesus' simple way to talk to His heaven Father while He was here on the earth. He goes into the wilderness to pray. He goes up the mountain top to spend time in prayer. He prays late at night, He starts off the morning with prayer. His life is saturated with prayer. It is never seen as a duty. It is never seen as a mere ritual. It was seen as a special time with His Heavenly Father.

And when His disciples ask Him to teach them to pray, He does it in an unusual way. He uses only around 65 words depending on your translation of Matthew 6:9-13. 55 words. You and I can repeat them in about 30 seconds if we talk fast enough. 30 seconds and we are good for the day. That is the way we can do it if we only look at prayer as some kind of duty that we are to simply check off. Got that done, now let's go out and face the day.

But is that what Jesus was really doing? We read in Luke 6:12 and other passages it was very common for Jesus to spend several hours, even all night in prayer. What did He say during all that time and why didn't He record for us one of those prayers? The longest prayer we have of Jesus' is John 17. And again you can say it in mere minutes. Why did Jesus share with us such a brief prayer when we know he spent hours with His Father?

I think it is because Jesus knew us all so well. We humans love to create lists, we love to create codes of laws and then over time enlarge. God gave us the 10 commandments, very simple and straightforward. However, in no time the ancient Jewish leaders enlarged those 10 to include at least 613 other commandments. And then later on added even more on top of the 613 to make sure that everyone knew exactly how to live according to the 613.

Remember what Jesus did? He took all 613 and even the 10 and reduced them to two simple commandments: *"And he answered, 'You shall love the LORD your God with all your heart and with all your soul and with all your strength and with all your mind, and your neighbor as yourself." (ESV)*

Jesus made it simple because it is simple. He did that with the commandments and he did that with prayer. Prayer is not to be complicated, it is God and us having a conversation.

But surely we must have an agenda. Don't we also need a way to measure our prayers? How else will we know that they are being answered? How else will we know that are doing any good? We need a prayer agenda, we need a way to measure our prayer times and its results. After all isn't it results that we are most after? Isn't the name of the game getting answers to our prayers? Aren't we wanting to pray effective prayers?

Again, Dr. Richard Foster helps us here by reminding us, "... *prayer is nothing more than an ongoing and growing love relationship with God the Father, Son and Holy Spirit.*" Notice the words "ongoing" and "growing love relationship". Nothing less, nothing more.

There is no secret formula except that of an open heart, a willing and obedient spirit. That is the key, being continually in prayer and knowing that it is through open communication with God that we grow in love, love for Him and for others.

Brother Lawrence understood this more than most. A little man who so wanted to be a man of God. For years he worked in the kitchen of a monastery. Just doing all he could do to help the monks that lived there at the time. He had no claim to fame. Just a simple man who started doing a simple thing. He spent his days in prayer. As much as he could throughout the day, he would converse with the LORD.

No big prayers that would cause others to notice him, but just an on and off prayer time throughout the day. It was his belief that God's Spirit wanted to be with his spirit. And therefore one could talk to the LORD washing dishes and taking out the trash as well as one could kneeling at the altar. It wasn't that he did not revere prayer. Quite the contrary, he elevated prayer. To him, prayer was a love relationship with God that was to be experienced throughout the day. It was not something that was to just be done at a certain time and then not practiced until the next day. No, prayer was open all day and one could talk with God all day long.

Did that mean he did not spend quality time in prayer? No, Brother Lawrence was very careful to have scheduled prayer times. He just did not end them once he left his room or the church. He was bold enough to believe that God wanted to spend the day with Him. And so, he acted on that belief and spend every day with God.

All that time with God transformed Bro. Lawrence. Something happened on the inside of him that poured out through his everyday life. His words found power. His mind gained knowledge and he possessed wisdom far beyond that of a simple man. It was not long after he began to live this way that suddenly people started coming to get his advice. Just a simple man who decided to walk with God and talk with Him throughout the day. Just a simple man who understood that prayer is simply an "ongoing and growing love relationship with the LORD."

4. **Prayer always leads to transformation**.

   Most of us start with ourselves as the subject and the center of our prayers. That is to say, usually when we pray it is more about us than about anything or anyone else. But as we progress with the LORD something wonderful happens. We begin to trust more and more in the LORD. We begin to understand that God will always meet our needs and so we begin to see a shift in the gravity of our souls. We become a prayer warrior for others. We join the ranks of those like Daniel and Job who not only prayed for themselves but became great intercessors for their family and friends.

   The deeper our prayer lives the deeper our love is for the LORD. The deeper our love is for the LORD the more we trust, the more we walk in faith. The more we walk in faith the more we understand His Power and Presence. We begin to understand just how much He loves us, cares for us and provides for us.

   The deeper our prayers lives are the more we are free to pray for others. And that becomes our joy. To spend time with the LORD in behalf of others. To join with Job as he prays for his children, for their salvation and blessing. To join with Daniel as he prays for his national leaders and his people. To join with Paul as he prays for those who will read his words, for their joy to be made complete. To join with Isaiah and ask to be a partner with the LORD in sharing His Word. To join with our Savior and laying ourselves at the feet of our LORD, saying "not my will, but yours be done."

5. **Be ready to experience the Supernatural**

One of the things that we can be assured of as we pray is that we will experience the supernatural. You cannot spend time with the LORD without experiencing His glory, majesty and grace. It is impossible.

Prayer moves mountains. Prayer changes the courses of people's lives. Prayer opens up the very windows of heaven. It is through prayer we are saved. It is through prayer we experience sanctification. It is through prayer that we are filled with His Holy Spirit. It is through prayer that we experience joy, peace and life.

In closing, always remember p prayer is talking to the LORD and He is a Person. God is not a what but a who. God is not a thing but as Martin Buber correctly states it we are to have an I and Thou relationship with the LORD.

God designed us for relationship. First with Him and then with others. In fact, He designed us to be with Him while we are with others. It the oneness Jesus was praying about in John 17. Remember?

And so our prayers should in time become conversations between friends. One of the greatest little joys of the play, Fiddler on the Roof, is the interplay between God and Tevye. It is more than just a man talking to God. It is a friend talking to a friend. It is a friend who knows the sacredness of God, who respects God but who is so comfortable with God that he can talk to him as friend to friend. So, too can we.

So, right now take 10 minutes or more and begin to talk to the LORD. If that feels odd, take out some paper and write out your prayers. Look and read the Psalms and understand many of them are just prayers put to music. Read John 17, Daniel 9, Matthew 6 and Paul's prayers to his different churches and friends. Check out E. M. Bounds writings on prayer (Power through Prayer), Philip Yancy book simply entitled <u>PRAYER</u>, Beth Moore's excellent little book on <u>Praying God's Word</u> and don't forget Richard Foster's book again simply titled <u>Prayer</u>. And of course there are literally hundreds of others that you could read from the pens of Bill Hybels, Andrew Murray, Watchman Nee and of course Oswald Chambers along with the likes of Theresa of Avila or Brother Lawrence.

But in the end here is the truth. You can read all the millions of pages dedicated to prayer and still not understand prayer in its entirety. You could get a PhD in the study of prayer and still be a prayer novice.

For prayer is more about practice than it is about study and theory. Foster in his book distinguishes between 21 different types of prayers and yet he would be the first to say there are many more and there are none. For prayer is not just something to be studied but it is something to be realized. Prayer is something to be experienced. Prayer is relational in essence.

And for that you don't need a lot of books, a great deal of study. For that all you need to do is open your heart and begin. Allow the Holy Spirit to lead you. Take the focus off of the amount of time. Take the focus off of your list. Simply begin talking with the LORD and then wait for Him to respond. Prayer is simply learning how to listen and respond, listen and learn, listen and rejoice. Listen and receive. Listen and obey. Listen and celebrate.

Will God talk to you? If He doesn't wouldn't that make you seem a little off balance? For he or she who starts to pray without expecting God to respond is a person perhaps who is in need of some medication or at least some serious counseling. Why pray if you don't expect God to communicate?

Our LORD Jesus shares with us that He heard His Heavenly Father. Noah hears God. Abraham heard God. Moses heard God. Peter, James and John heard God. Lydia, Dorcas, Mary and Sarah all heard God. We will hear from God as well, all it takes is an open heart and an obedient spirit.

Let me leave you with one more quote before we venue into working as a partner with God. It is from Jonna Weaver's book, <u>Having a Mary Heart in a Martha World.</u> She is quoting Kent Hughes, *"Our lives are like photographic plates, and prayer is like a time exposure to God. As we expose ourselves to God for a half hour, an hour, perhaps two hours a day, his image in imprinted more and more upon us. More and more we absorb the image of his character, his love, his wisdom, his way of dealing with life and people."*

Today, allow God to imprint Himself more and more on and through your life. WOW, what a great God we serve. Now, turn the page and we will continue our adventure into growing deeper in the LORD.

Note - For those who would like a more detailed look at all the spiritual disciplines let me encourage you to read Richard Foster's book <u>CELEBRATION OF DISCIPLINE</u> or Dallas Willard's book, <u>THE GREAT OMMISSION</u> for starters. These are two of the finest books ever written on the spiritual disciplines and they have been a great service and joy to me and my walk with Christ.

Also at the end of this book is an example of the Tabernacle Prayer made famous by Pastor Cho. It has been adapted to fit a particular congregation. However, you can adapt it to fit your needs as well.

CHAPTER THREE - PARTNERING WITH GOD
A Rejection of the Pareto Principle

"After this the LORD appointed seventy two others and sent them on ahead of him, two by two, into every town and place where he himself was about to go. And He said to them, 'The harvest is plentiful, but the laborers are few. Therefore prayer earnestly to the Lord of the harvest to send out laborers into his harvest." - Luke 10:1-2 (ESV)

"Moses' father-in-law said to him, 'What you are doing is not good, You and the people with you will certainly wear yourselves out, for the thing is too heavy for you. You are not able to do it alone." - Exodus 18:17-18

"You are the light of the world. A city set on a hill cannot be hidden. No do people light a lamp and put it under a basket, but on a stand, and it gives light to all in the house. In the same way, let your light shine before others, so that they may see your good works and give glory to your Father who is in heaven." - Matthew 5:14-16

We now come to a key step in a person's spiritual journey with the LORD. The step of going from a life of "receiving and feeding" to a life of "partnering and serving." Let's recap our steps so far, understanding again, that all these steps can interweave and overlap.

1. We all start off in the "WORLD CROWD". We all start off as members of the fallen human race. We are dead in our sins and alienated from God. (Romans 3:23)

2. Through the work of the Holy Spirit we are invited to become "watchers and listeners." We are drawn to watch and listen to the leadings of the LORD. We become part of the crowd that is drawn to the LORD. (Romans 1:19-21)

3. The more we watch and listen, the more we are drawn to Jesus. The more we see Him, experience Him, the more we understand that Jesus can meet all of our needs. We join those, like the 5,000, who understood that Jesus can truly meet all of our needs. We deepen our relationship with Jesus to that of being a "receiver and feeder." We understand that it is through Jesus that we can have all our needs met and we bow before Him to receive Him.

4. It is here that Jesus wants us to draw even closer. It is right here that God invites us into a very special relationship, the relationship of partnership. God calls us into a life of service. He calls us from a mere live of passivity to an active life of service and partnership.

From the moment Adam took his first breath he came into a life of partnership with God. Genesis tells us that Adam worked with the LORD in the garden, among the flowers and trees, and among all of nature. Adam was not a passive creature. He was enthusiastically working with God, creating God's Kingdom here on earth.

With the arrival of Eve that partnership was not dissolved. Instead, it was further enhanced. Now, together as man and wife, Adam and Eve would be co-partners with the LORD. Now it would be a partnership of three – God, Adam, and Eve. Together, they would bring about God's kingdom, God's will on earth.

The idea of partnering with the LORD is both primordial and an essential part of our DNA. It has always been God's desire to work alongside us. It has always been His desire for there to be this relationship where we advance from mere "receiving and feeding" to one of "partnering and serving".

There comes a point in our walk with the LORD that we are invited to being more than just feeders. This is exactly the Apostle Paul's challenge to the Church at Corinth. They had accepted Jesus as their Savior, and they had, in earnest, begun their walk with Him. But, somewhere along the way they had stopped growing. They had gone from being mere "watchers and listeners" to becoming "receivers and feeders." However, it was at this stage in their spiritual walk that they became stagnate. Listen to Paul's words:

"But I, brothers, could not address you as spiritual people, but as people of the flesh, as infants in Christ. I fed you with milk, not solid food, for you were not ready for it. And even now you are not yet ready, for you are still in the flesh. For while there is jealousy and strife among you, are you not of the flesh and behaving only in a human way?" (1 Corinthians 3:1-3 ESV).

Paul's struggle was real. He wanted more than just a milk bottle relationship for the Corinthians. He knew if they remain in such a state that they would always suffer from strife and jealousy, and in turn they would begin to stagnate, decay and eventually die. Paul was fighting for their very survival. Paul was doing his best to wake them up before it was too late.

We, too, are challenged to be more than "babes" only able to suckle spiritual milk. We are called to experience an "Isaiah" moment. That is a moment when we step into the ministry ourselves. A moment when we begin to actively use our gifts to help others. The moment when we go from drinking spiritual milk to setting the table for others, filled with all kinds of spiritual food.

In Isaiah chapter six we read about Isaiah's heavenly vision. *"In the year that King Uzziah died I saw the LORD sitting upon a throne, high and lifted up; and the train (hem) of his robe filled the temple. Above Him stood the seraphim. Each had six wings; with two he covered his face, and with two he covered his feet, and with two he flew. And one called to another and said: 'Holy, holy, holy is the LORD of hosts; the whole earth is full of his glory.'" (Isaiah 6:1-3* ESV).

Isaiah is taken aback. He is in the presence of God Almighty completely overwhelmed. All around him is God's Majesty, Power, and Holiness. Why has the LORD appeared to him, a man who calls himself "a man of unclean lips"? Isaiah is rightly afraid for his life. How can he, an unclean man, be in this place of holiness? Is his death now inevitable? Is this the end of life?

No, it is only the beginning for Isaiah. For what we read is about in the next few words is God's graciousness and God's invitation. God reaches out to Isaiah to deepen their relationship and to invite him into a partnership.

Did God not know that this man possessed "unclean lips"? Did God not know this man's, or any man's for that matter, frailties and failures? Of course God did! The LORD is fully aware of all our problems, our failures, our sins; but, God is always inviting us to be with Him. He knew all about Isaiah, but He desired more than anything to talk to Isaiah, to spend time with Isaiah. Isaiah had not somehow stormed heaven or snuck into heaven to experience this vision. No, God had graciously opened up a window of heaven and was inviting Isaiah a little peek. All that we read in chapter six has been initiated by the LORD, Himself. But it was more than Isaiah was able to comprehend. His mind kept coming back to the fact that he was full of sin. How could he, a man of sin, ever have a partnership with GOD? And so, God just reaches down and alleviates Isaiah's problems. Isaiah centers on the sinfulness of his lips (his speech, his life). So, God simply sanctifies those lips with Holy fire and now with that out of the way, they can talk. Sin gone, guilt gone, problem solved. Now let's talk.

That is the way it is with God. We tend to worry so much about our own unworthiness we allow it to become a barrier between us and the LORD. God knows our issues. And God knows that He can take care of all of our issues. Whatever it is that causes you problems, just give it to God. He will take care of it. For Isaiah it was having guilt, having "unclean lips." No big problem for the LORD. Confessed, God made his lips holy, sanctified, ready for service. Whatever it is that causes you issues, God is ready to cleanse, to sanctify, and to make you ready for His service.

And what does the LORD and Isaiah talk about? They talk about going into partnership. They talk about Isaiah going into the service of the LORD. God gives out a general call of "who will work with me to share my warnings and my message with My People"? Who will take My words to them? Who will work with Me?

Isaiah immediately responds in verse 9 - "*HERE I AM! SEND ME.*" Here I am, the one You have just made holy. The one You just cleansed from all their sin and guilt. The one who has seen Your glory. It was not out of some emotional high point that Isaiah makes this commitment. Service, partnership, is simply -- the natural response of a person who has been transformed by the LORD.

The whole Bible is full of such stories. Stories of those who have been transformed by the LORD in turn become partners with Him in the Kingdom. Those that connect with the LORD area able to bear fruit. Those that are Spirit filled take up the Great Commission in their hearts and through their daily lives.

Need a New Testament story? Need a story that doesn't involve a holy priest? Okay. How about a regular Joe that becomes a great ambassador for the LORD? A man who wasn't even part of the 72 or even the 12 that we are aware.

How about a man called Barnabas? You find his story throughout the book of Acts. Spiritually, Barnabas had decided to do more than just listen and watch Jesus. He began to actively follow Jesus. And for a good amount of the time he was a part of the "receive and feed" crowd. He saw Jesus as the One who can meet all his needs. But, beginning in Acts 4, we see a Barnabas that has stepped up his relationship with the LORD. He goes from just a man who believes that we need to "receive and feed" to one who is decides to take up God's invitation of serving and partnering. He decides that he wants to dine on more than just the "milk" of the Gospel. He is ready for some spiritual steak and potatoes.

Acts 4:32 - 37 tells us that Barnabas surrenders some land that he owns into the hands of the LORD. The land is to be sold with the proceeds to be used for the needs of the less fortunate. He puts the earnings of the sale at the feet of the Apostles so that they can use it for the Kingdom of God.

Barnabas displays to us one way to partner with the LORD. God had graciously given this certain field to Barnabas. It was a part of his heritage. To the Jews land meant everything. Land was sacred. Land was holy. It was a gift of God for His Promise People.

But Barnabas knew in his spirit that he was not the real owner of this land. Barnabas knew that he was only the steward. This land was first and foremost God's. Although he held the earthly title, the land was the LORD's. So, when the LORD whispered to Barnabas that it was time for the land to be sold to another, Barnabas immediately partnered with God. He did not hesitate. He did not argue or complain. And when the LORD further whispered to Barnabas to give the money to the Apostles, Barnabas agreed. He took his hands off of it. He placed it into the hands of the Apostles.

It is easy to read this little passage and miss the full ramifications. This was not just the selling of land like we do here in America. This was the giving of up of one's heritage. This was the transfer of land that no doubt had been in Barnabas' family for generations. This was a "Pearl of Great Price" possession. And yet, Barnabas is able to graciously and willingly give this gift away. How? Why? It is all because Barnabas knew it was time to step up and become a partner with the LORD. And in his case, it meant to sell the land and let its proceeds go to help others.

And that is not all, for we witness Barnabas not only partnering with God, he also partners with the Apostles. Barnabas puts his faith in the LORD and he puts his faith in the Apostles. That, my friend is the joy of true partnering with the LORD. It is when we partner with others together for His Kingdom, when we come together in partnership with God and one another to bring about God's Kingdom here on earth. That can only be done if we are willing to grow deeper. If we are willing to go from just being "receivers and feeders" to being "partners and servers" for the LORD. Oh, how desperate we need churches, families, and individuals today that will see beyond their own needs and partner with God to bring about His Kingdom.

We see later that Barnabas goes on to do some amazing things for others and for the Kingdom of God. At first, it was partnering with the

LORD in the sale of some dirt, later it would be giving to the LORD some years of his life to tell others about Jesus.

The book of Acts also tells us that it was Barnabas that was used to bring Saul/Paul into the ministry of Jesus. No one believed that Saul/Paul had been transformed. His reputation was horrendous! But, God used Barnabas much the same way that God used the angel to heal Isaiah, to bring Paul into good favor with the Early Church. Barnabas was God's agent to declare Paul's conversion to the New Way. Is there any wonder when Luke wants to describe Barnabas that he uses the following description that we find in Acts 11:24 *"for he was a good man, full of the HOLY SPIRIT and of faith. And a great many people were added to the LORD."* Acts 11:24 (ESV)

Barnabas did not just stop with Paul. For it was Barnabas that the LORD partnered with that helped pave the way for the Early Church to reach out to the Gentiles. It was Barnabas that the LORD partnered with that rescued a timid young disciple named John Mark, who would later write, of course, the Gospel of Mark.

All of this happened because Barnabas took the next step of service, of partnering and serving with the LORD. All of this happened because he stepped out of a "5,000 relationship" to be a part of a mighty movement for the LORD. He went beyond "receiving and feeding" to "partnering and serving".

It is a step that we are all called to take. It is the step of taking our light and letting it shine for the LORD. It is the step in which we don't just come around Jesus to "receive and feed", but we want to be a part of the 70/72, we want to be a part of God's partnership team.

It is at this point in our walk where we begin to ask ourselves some very important questions:

- What can I do to serve Jesus, the Savior and LORD of my life? He has done so much for me, He is doing so much for me, now how can I serve Him?
- What gifts, talents and resources do I have that will help the Kingdom of God?
- Just how much can I provide so that others can come to Christ or to have their physical needs? How much can I sacrifice so that others will not have to sacrifice?
- In what ways can I be "salt and light" for the LORD?

This time of searching and asking such questions could be labeled "connection time". That time when we realize that we are connected to Jesus to do more than just "receive and feed." John 15 shows us the way: *"I am the true vine, and my Father is the vinedresser. Every branch in me that does not bear fruit he takes away, and every branch that does bear fruit he prunes, that it may bear more fruit."* John 15:1-3 (ESV).

We begin to understand that there is much more in store for us than just being connected. We are connected for a purpose. Yes, to save our soul; but, just as importantly to become all that we can become. And in the case of the vine of course that is to bear fruit. And in our case the same is also true, we are to bear the fruit of God. We call it the fruit of the Holy Spirit. Paul in Galatians 5:22-23 shares with us what that fruit looks life. He defines it this way, *"... the fruit of the*

Spirit is love, joy, peace, patience, kindness, goodness, faithfulness, gentleness, self-control; against such things there is no law."

Look back over that list. One of the things that you notice very quickly is the fact that all of those characteristics, those traits, those attributes require a relationship. True love is agape love. Love that is shared, love that is a part of a relationship. Joy is the same. In fact, all of fruit of the Holy Spirit are partnership words, all of them are sharing words. Our God designed it that way. He knows that the only way we can bear fruit is through connection, through a partnership with Him. He desires for us to "receive and feed," but then to partner with Him in service to produce fruit.

In Luke 10:25 - 37, Jesus further punctuates this fact in sharing the Parable of the Good Samaritan. Notice in verse 34 as Luke describes the actions of the man - *"He went to him and bound up his wounds, pouring on oil and wine."*

Along with a heart of compassion, the Good Samaritan had a prepared heart of compassion. He well understood the dangers of the Jericho Road. It was a byway for muggers and murderers. Any unsuspecting person was a potential victim to be taken advantage of and mobbed. The Good Samaritan was well aware of all these fact. And so, as a frequent traveler he put some things on his donkey that he might need, some bandages and oil for healing and wine. He wanted to be prepared as he traveled along.

Jesus tells us that he was prepared to help the man before he even saw him. He already was prepared to be "salt and light" to any that needed it. This story is more than just the story of a person ready to help. It is a call to all those who want to be a part of this next relationship with the LORD, this next step to be a person ready to serve others.

Today, we would call this man a first responder, and like all first responders, he was not only willing, he was prepared. He came with the right heart, the right skill and the right equipment.
He was able to take a man who could not help himself and assist him back to health. I love Jesus' words at the end of the story - *"You go, and do likewise."* That is our call to service, to partner with the LORD. We are commissioned to take our lives and begin to pour them out into the lives of others. Like Isaiah, the LORD is asking, Who will go for us?

But what about us? I mean, if we use part of our time to take care of the needs of others, will we not forsake the time that we need to take care of ourselves? If we are dedicated to taking care of the needs of others, who will take care of us?

Funny you should ask. Jesus gives us the answer for that. Let's go back to John chapter four with the Woman at the Well. If you remember, Jesus was so hungry and thirsty that He just had to stop. He couldn't go any further. He sent the rest of the disciples on to get some food and bring Him back what they could find.

How long it took, we do not know. But in verse 31 after the event the disciples are doing their best to get Jesus to eat the food that they had bought and yet, Jesus tells them He is full. Did He hide a holy snickers bar somewhere? Has the woman at the well slipped Him a protein bar?

What happened was Jesus had been supernaturally feed by His Heavenly Father. *"My food is to do the will of Him who sent me and to accomplish his work."* In other words, Jesus knew that the Father would take care of Him and His Father did take care of Him. How the Father did it we don't know. We just know that in doing the will of the Father, Jesus' needs were met.

That is exactly how all of our needs will be met. As we connect with the LORD in partnership, God not only allows us to meet the needs of others, our own needs are met as well. It's a supernatural reality. What happened for Jesus can happen for us as well. All we have to do is to be ready to partner with the LORD.

But what can I do? I mean, I don't have the right skill set. I don't know enough and I really just need to sit and learn more and more. I need to be a sponge, not a food server. I need to grow so more before I got out to partner and serve. I need more time. I am not ready. I, I, I.

We have to reject such poor thinking. The reality is this, we can discover ways to serve and partner with the LORD. First and foremost we can all pray. We can all intercede for others. Secondly, we can all give a part of our time and a portion of our resources. We can all find ways to help others. It has been said that most of the work in any organization is done by only 20%. If that is the truth, then it is a shame.

History shows us that great things can be accomplished when people come together. That was never truer than in World War II. Everyone one from young children to mothers to working men and women, along with soldiers, all partnered together to win the war. Victory gardens were planted to meet the needs of the army. People fasted and rationed their goods so that others might have something to eat. Women went to work building ships and planes so that the men could take up arms and fight the battle. Everyone had a part to play, and because of great sacrifice, all that service and willingness to partner, a great evil was stopped in our world and peace was obtained.

We are now facing an even greater evil. An evil that will not just enslave the bodies of men and women and boys and girls, but one that will enslave the souls of all mankind. We are facing an onslaught of demonic proportions. The very souls of millions are at stake. We live at a time when there is an all out attack on Christianity and following Jesus.

The question is will we stand up to the task. Will we join together as the Body of Christ and co-partner with one another to defeat Satan and all evil? We have been promised victory, but only if we connect with God and do our part. Satan cannot stop the advance of the Kingdom of God. However, we can choose not to pray, not to partner with God and not to serve. We can choose to "*desert Him who called you in the grace of God*" (Galatians 1:6 ESV). We can choose to desert and we will be overrun by evil and our culture will look more like hell than the Kingdom of God.

Jesus did not send out lone rangers. Instead, He created strength through companionship. Jesus sent out His disciples two by two and they came back with great joy. Together they had defeated Satan, they had brought healing and wholeness into the lives of those that they met. Together they were a means of transformation for many of the villages and towns that they shared the message of Jesus. Together they fought against the powers of evil and were victorious.

The plan of God is rather simple. God saves us, redeems us, so that we can partner with Him and others in bringing that message of salvation to others in need. We are called to fulfill the Great Commission (Matthew 28:16-20). God will provide the way. Just as the angel told Gideon, "*The LORD is with you, mighty warrior*" (Judges 6:12), we need to realize that the LORD is with us to serve and share the gospel of Jesus.

Today, let me ask you - where are you working? What are you actively doing for the Kingdom of Jesus? You may not be called to a specialized ministry, but you are called to be a part of the priesthood of all believers. In other words you are called to do your part. At the very least, that means to be faithful in your attendance at your local church and small group (see Hebrews 10:25).   At the very least, that means to be a pray warrior for others (2 Thessalonians 3:1-5). At the very least, that means to be a partner in supporting God's Kingdom (Galatians 6:1-10).

For there is a massive need around us. Jesus tells us that by telling us that we are surrounded by a great harvest. We don't have to look very far to find people who need help. All around there are needy people.

One of our great modern sins is the reality that there is a meager amount of people willing to work for the Kingdom, but that does not have to be true in your life. You do not have to be a part of the silent majority. No, like Isaiah, like Barnabas, like generations before us, we can choose to accept the LORD's invitation to come out of the 5,000 and join the 72 in partnering with the LORD. In being a vital part of those that as Robert Crosby puts in his book, <u>THE ONE WHO JESUS LOVES</u> (page116-117):

1. Travel light. To follow Jesus farther, we have to lay aside the things that will weigh us down and hold us back in our pursuit of Him and his work.
2. Stay focused. We must determine with every opportunity, is it a divine appointment or a diversion?
3. Cultivate the Faithful Ones. "Show me your five closest friends and I'll show you where you will be in five years." - quote from Carl Lentz.
4. Minister to people's felt needs.
5. Proclaim the Great Day has come.

You and I have been invited to be partners with the LORD. To be active in ministry. To be prayer warriors, to be givers, to be ambassadors. For some of us it will be life changing, for others it will be just a part of our everyday life. Are you ready to step up and become more than just a "receiver and feeder"? I hope so, because there is even more in store for those who will take this step of "partnering with the LORD", of being a servant for Jesus.

What is the more? Jesus is calling us to experience an ever deeper walk with Him, one that was modeled best by the 12. But, before we talk about that, let's look at another of the Spiritual Disciplines. This is the discipline of Fasting.

However, before we do that, we need to put to rest one of the biggest myths that is affecting our world today, especially those of us inside the Church. It is a myth that originated out of the world of economics. It has been labeled the *Pareto Principle* or what some call the 80/20 rule.

The **Pareto principle** simply states that, for many events, roughly 80% of the effects come from 20% of the causes. Joseph M. Juran, a management specialists suggested the principle and named it after Italian economist Vilfredo Pareto. Pareto while at the University of Lausanne in 1896, published a paper entitled "Cours d' economie politique." (COURSE OF POLITICAL ECONOMY) Essentially, Pareto showed that approximately 80% of the land in Italy was owned by 20% of the population. He then developed the principle by observing that 20% of the pea pods in his garden contained 80% of the peas. From this, he theorized that 80% of the actual work was completed by the 20%.

And from that theory others began to look at other areas especially in the areas of manufacturing and sales and concluded the following:

- 80% of a company's profits come from 20% of its customers
- 80% of a company's complaints come from 20% of its customers
- 80% of a company's profits come from 20% of the time its staff spend
- 80% of a company's sales come from 20% of its products
- 80% of a company's sales are made by 20% of its sales staff

People took the theory and have attempted to push it as fact. However, what exists in the world can never be used as a template for the Kingdom of God. For far too long we have taken the word of a single man and what seems to appear in manufacturing and sales and have said therefore, that the same must exist in the Church, in the Kingdom of God. So, if we can get 20% of the congregation engaged, then we have done the best that can be done. We must accept the 80/20 rule in the Kingdom of God.

However, you do not find this 80/20 principle in Scripture. What you do find is when we sow like Jesus tells us in the Parable of the soils, we will face some soil that will be too hard, other soil that will produce both weeds and plants. In other words, we will face difficulty. But we also see that in the good soil, we don't have a 20/80 principle we have such words as thirty fold, sixty fold and a hundred fold. We have exponential growth.

That is kingdom language. So, while you can be cognizant of Pareto's Principle, do not allow it to cause you to be dismayed or to be discouraged. In your own life dig as deep as you can in your relationship with the LORD, knowing that the better soil that you are, instead of 20/80, is more like 30/60/100 fold. And the better soil you have in your church, the more supernatural growth you are going to experience. You are going to see more than just a handful digging deep and growing in the LORD. It is going to be an explosion of growth.

After all according to Pareto's Principle, at best we should have meager results from what happened on Pentecost. After all, only 120 were filled with the Spirit. But, if I read correctly, Acts 2 tells us that some 3,000 were added to the Kingdom that day. It is high time we understand the world's advice, but it is also high time that we understand that in the power and presence of the HOLY SPIRIT we can experience miracles and wonders too amazing to understand and comprehend. We are not condemned to live by an 80/20 principle. We are invited to experience supernatural exponential growth.

"Now to Him who is able to do far more abundantly that all we ask or think according to the power at work within us, to Him be glory in

the church and in Christ Jesus throughout all generations, forever and ever. Amen." - Ephesians 3:20-21 (ESV)

Now, let's go look at the Spiritual Discipline of Fasting.

SPIRITUAL DISCIPLINE # 3
FASTING

And when they had ordained them elders in every church, and had prayed with fasting, they commended them to the Lord, on whom they believed. (Acts 14:23)

Matthew 6:16-18 "And when you fast, do not look gloomy like the hypocrites, for they disfigure their faces that their fasting may be seen by others. Truly, I say to you, they have received their reward. But when you fast, anoint your head and wash your face that your fasting may not be seen by others but by your Father who is in secret. And your Father who sees in secret will reward you."

Isaiah 56:3-7 "Why have we fasted, and you see it not? Why have we humbled ourselves, and you take no knowledge of it?' Behold, in the day of your fast you seek your own pleasure, and oppress all your workers. Behold, you fast only to quarrel and to fight and to hit with a wicked fist. Fasting like yours this day will not make your voice to be heard on high. Is such the fast that I choose, a day for a person to humble himself? Is it to bow down his head like a reed, and to spread sackcloth and ashes under him? Will you call this a fast, and a day acceptable to the Lord? "Is not this the fast that I choose: to loose the bonds of wickedness, to undo the straps of the yoke, to let the oppressed go free, and to break every yoke? Is it not to share your bread with the hungry and bring the homeless poor into your house;

when you see the naked, to cover him and not to hide yourself from your own flesh?"

Dr. Richard Foster defines fasting this way: "The central idea in fasting is the voluntary denial of an otherwise normal function for the sake of intense spiritual activity. There is nothing wrong with any normal life-functions; it is simply that there are times when we set them aside in order to concentrate." (Study Guide for Celebration of Discipline, page 28).

Fasting does at times involve food, the Bible shares that reality with us. But, it can mean a great deal more. It can mean for instance:

1. **Fasting from people.** This involves a fast usually called solitude. It enables us a time to be away from the crowd so that we can return more ready to love and serve.

2. **Fasting from media and other distractions.** Yes, this includes cell phones, iPods, social media, along with all other forms of media. Not because they are inherently evil, which they are not, but because we need some "Sabbath time" away from these forms of instant communication. In the past, one of the great rewards from summer church camps was when our children came back overjoyed with the news that "GOD SPOKE TO ME!" What happened at camp in those days involved the fact that there was a set amount of time when we were to be without any media of any kind and we were secluded and had uninterrupted time to read from the Word, pray, and be in worshipful fellowship with others. We were simply free of

enough distractions for a long time period that we were able to hear the LORD speaking.

Sadly, today that is not the case. And it is also not the case that many of our young people are able to hear from the LORD or that we are able to hear from the LORD. *Be still and know that I am God* is still in Scripture. God will not always shout to us, just ask Elijah. More often than not, He whispers. So, in order to hear Him, it requires us, at times, to turn off the electronics and get quiet before our LORD.

3. **Fasting from consumerism.** We live in a culture in which we can usually get what we want, when we want it. For our soul's sake, we need times when we practice going without things. When we take the time to realize that much of the world goes without all of our "stuff." most of the time. It is not a time of self-righteous judgment, but a time when we humbly go without obtaining more stuff, more things that one day will only rust and become garage sale treasures. It is a time when we realize that our life is not all the stuff we accumulate. Our lives are much richer than crass materialism. It will also help us to learn from those who still find balance in not having everything. It is a time for us to put away all the advertisements, to turn our eyes away from all the billboards and instead to turn our eyes toward our Savior and see where we can use those resources to help others in need.

If we are not careful we become so insensitive to the needs of our global friends that we forget their basic needs for our needs of a new toy, a new gun, shoe, etc. when our closets and our tool boxes, along with our garages are overfilled with things that we don't even remember buying.

That is not to say that we must, like St. Francis, get rid of everything and walk the rest of our lives barefoot. However, it also does not mean that we live like the Rich Fool of Luke 12:16-21 who suddenly had a rather unpleasant encounter with the LORD. We are to live a life of balance, of enjoying the riches that God so graciously gives to all of us, while at the same time reaching out and making sure that we meet the needs of others around the world.

4.   **Fasting from food**. In a culture that is dotted with fine dining restaurants and fast food, fasting seems so out of place. Why in the world, with food being offered at every corner, would we even want to deny ourselves food? Why, that would be un-American!

If you believe all the hype, you can even begin to argue that going without three meals a day, along with a snack or two can injure your health. At least, that is what the world wants us to believe. But the reality is, while we can only go a few days without water, we can go up to 40 days without food, and rarely, has the LORD asked anyone to go 40 days without food. What we are talking about normally is going without food for a day or for a single meal.

Scripture has so much to say about fasting that it would take an entire book just to study all the passages. A list of those who practiced fasting is a literally Who's who of spiritual giants.

Spiritual giants such as, Moses along with David, Esther, Elijah, Ann, Daniel, and of course, our Savior Jesus. Just the fact that Jesus fasted should be enough information for us to understand that fasting should be a part of our spiritual life.

Now, there are some things that we need to say upfront about going without food.

1. We don't fast for weight loss. There is nothing wrong in this type of fasting; in fact, it might be good for us to fast from some foods so that our bodies become more in balance, healthier.

2. And we do not go on a hunger fast to twist the arms of God. Like we could if we wanted to, right? Biblical, spiritual discipline fasting is tied to one's spirituality.

Biblical fasting is practiced for physical, emotional, relational, and spiritual cleansing and for aligning our lives and our hearts to our LORD. Fasting has to do more with what it will do in our own lives rather in the lives of those around us. God at times uses fasting to get our attention, to help us find balance in our everyday lives. And today, we need more balance than ever.

In Scripture the normal means of fasting involved abstaining from all food, solid or liquid for a set amount of time. One was permitted, and even encouraged, to drink water. Only rarely was abstinence from water to be observed.

It is true that our LORD Jesus practiced a 40 day fast. However, this kind of fast is normally quite unusual and should only be done when one is overwhelmingly convinced that it is a directive from the LORD. Most fasts were of this type of scale:

1. Individuals practiced "absolute fasting" - this would include the abstinence of both water and food. This was not the normal method of fasting. It was only done in unusual circumstances. For example, an absolute fast was practiced when there was a danger of Jewish genocide as in the story of Mordecai and Esther. Esther desired supernatural knowledge and favor before she approached her husband, the King of Persia. So, she along with her maidens practiced a three day absolute fast. (See Esther chapter 4 for more of the story.)

Others like Paul, Moses and Elijah practiced absolute fasts. But, they were far and few between. Again, one must be led by the Spirit to practice such fasting. (See Acts 9:9; Deut. 9:9 and 1 Kings 19:8).

2. The most usual form of fasting was the practice of going without food for a day or for a meal. This was the manner most often practiced. Usually a day without food was set aside for the Day of Atonement (Lev. 23:27). More often than not, it was a single meal that was given to the LORD as an offering of praise and thanksgiving.

Jesus, Himself, talks about this kind of fasting in the Sermon on the Mount. He promoted fasting, but not the kind that would in turn cause attention upon the one fasting. He encouraged fasting; but, to do it quietly, privately and without fanfare. (Matthew 6:16). Jesus was not replacing fasting. He was restoring a proper mindset and balance to fasting.

3.   Most fasts that have been recorded in the Bible and throughout Christian history have been individual in nature; although, Scripture does share with us that for a time of revival the whole population was encouraged to fast. (Joel 2:5; 1 Chronicles 20:1-4). In 1756, a rather interesting event surrounded a national fast encouraged by King George II.   The nation of Britain declared a fast asking for God to help them turn back an oncoming invasion of the French. The nation went both to prayer and to fasting.   Pastor John Wesley records this day of fasting in his journal with the following footnote as to the outcome of the period of fasting: "Humility was turned into national rejoicing for the threatened invasion by the French was averted."

So, are we to fast? Yes. But how? For how long? If we look towards both Scripture and history then I think we can safely make the following conclusions:

It appears that we are encouraged to take a day or two and fast either the whole day or one of its meals. That is, to go without food for a meal or for a portion of the day or for the whole day.   This seems to be what we see practiced both in the days of Zechariah (Zech. 18:12) and in the Early Church. The Didache (Early Church Teaching) urged disciples of Jesus to practice fasting on two days, Wednesdays and Fridays. John Wesley asked his Methodists to observe both of these days as a fast day. It was left up to the individual how they were to be practiced – to either to go the whole day or go without a meal or a portion of a meal.

The idea was not as much how much food we have to avoid, as to the spirit by which we are fasting. Jesus made this clear in His teachings. While there appears not to be a divine law binding us to fast, both Scripture and history shows us that it is through fasting that people have experienced growth. Prayers have been answered. Lives have been changed.

Fasting must forever center on the LORD. It must be both God-initiated and God-ordained. We are invited to join Anna (Luke 2:37) who practiced fasting as a part of her worship experience.

So, why fast? If we are not commanded to do it, we are only encouraged to do it - can't we just skip this fasting all together, and would you please pass the potatoes and gravy as we continue to talk?

More than any other single discipline, fasting seems to have this knack of revealing to us things that control us. When we are led by the Lord to fast either food, friends, media, or other things one of the effects is we begin to experience a more balanced lifestyle. This is one of the wonderful benefits of this discipline. It helps us to be more and more transformed into the image of Jesus.

When we fast, it is not uncommon for us to have to deal with such issues as pride, arrogance, selfishness, anger, jealousy, strife, fear, envy and the like in our lives. David said, "*I humbled my soul with fasting.*" Psalms 69:10.

Fasting helps us keep our lives, all of our lives in balance. I believe Dr. Gerald G. May is correct in his book, **Grace and Addiction**, when he said that we are, by human nature, susceptible to unbalance, susceptible to having addictions in our lives. Fasting helps us with our addictions. All of us suffer from the effects of allowing nonessentials to control our lives. We all too quickly have a craving for things that we do not need until those very things enslave us.

How many of us have ever taken up a hobby only to have that hobby begin to enslave us. All too often what happens is that we first begin to fish, then we get hooked, and pretty soon we are working longer hours to pay for all the equipment, the new truck we had to have to pull the boat. The more money we now need to fill the boat with fuel and the more money we need for new reels, bait, and license. What started off as a hobby has become a second job.

The same thing can happen in all areas of our lives, with clothing, with books, with tools, with cars, with shoes, with jewelry, and even with nails and tanning. We humans have a tendency to start off well with a hobby only to have that hobby take over our lives. Paul tells us, *"All things are lawful for me, but I will not be enslaved by anything."* (1 Corinthians 6:12).

So, how shall we start? Richard Foster in his book, <u>Celebration of Discipline</u>, gives us some helpful advice. Here is his advice:

- Begin wise - learn to walk before you run. Begin with a partial fast. This may mean one meal or up to two meals. Attempt this for a week or two. Use the normal time for eating as a time to rejoice and pray. Take a walk, get away from the kitchen or dining hall. Use the time to have communion with the LORD.

- Next, attempt a full day fast. From dinner time one evening till dinner time the next evening. Use only water, but plenty of it. Break your fast with a light meal of fresh fruits and vegetables and a good deal of inner rejoicing.

- Next, attempt a 36 hour fast or a three meal fast. With that accomplishment, it is time to seek the LORD as to whether He wants you to go on a longer fast. Three to seven days is a good time period and will probably have a substantial impact on the course of your life. However, please remember your motivation for going on a fast is to cleanse your mind, your heart and your soul. So, allow the LORD to direct you in knowing how to practice your fasting.

As you can see, the above advice is good not only for food, but also for other fasts as well. Try at first going a half a day without all the media, without being surrounded by people or whatever the LORD is trying to get you to fast. Then, little by little, more and more time until you being to experience more balance than ever in your life.

- There are some strict guidelines to longer fasting that are covered in Foster's book and I would encourage you to read his book. For most people, the norm will range from a one meal fast to a three day fast. If you are interested in knowing about longer fasts, I would encourage you to read his book, along with his book on prayer to prepare you for a longer time of fasting.

Now, what about those that can't food fast - diabetics, expectant mothers, or those who for physical reasons should not fast. Well, they can practice other fasts. It has not hurt any diabetic to fast a time of TV, Facebook, cell phone, or friends, and it has not hurt any diabetic under doctor's advice to fast a partial amount of a meal - to go without part of the meal.

Again, it is not the amount of food that is the key. It is the motive of the heart, the opening of the soul and the willingness to allow the LORD to help you truly find balance in your life. Fasting can bring breakthroughs in the spiritual realm that simply cannot happen any other way. It is a means of God's grace and blessing that we are encouraged not to neglect or avoid. It is my hope and prayer that however the LORD leads you to practice the spiritual discipline of fasting, it becomes a means of grace in your life, that fasting will serve as a means, as a way for you to experience a deeper walk with our LORD. And, that fasting enables you to possess an ever growing balance that will thereby lead you to be a more effective disciple of our LORD and Savior Jesus Christ. Now is the time for all of us to do all we can to hear the voice of Christ. For we all want to hear the words of Jesus say, 'Well done, thou good and faithful servant.' May fasting be one of the means for us to be able to hear and receive those words.

In closing this section, let's hear from some of those whose spiritual lives have been greatly enhanced by the spiritual discipline of fasting.

"If there is no element of asceticism in our lives, if we give free rein to the desires of the flesh (taking care of course to keep within the limits of what seems permissible to the world), we shall find it hard to train for the service of Christ. When the flesh is satisfied it is hard to pray with cheerfulness or to devote oneself to a life of service which calls for much self-renunciation." — Dietrich Bonhoeffer, The Cost of Discipleship

Fasting is abstaining from anything that hinders prayer. ~ Andrew Bonar, Minister, Free Church of Scotland

Fasting helps express, deepens, confirms the resolution that we are ready to sacrifice anything, even ourselves, to attain what we seek for the kingdom of God. ~ Andrew Murray, Missionary to South Africa

Once you have settled on the type of fast, commit to a day when you will fast and settle on the specific spiritual purpose of your fast. Next, confess to God any fear or anxiety related to fasting. Rather than merely setting aside a set day each week, you may also wish to commit to fast whenever prompted by the Holy Spirit, which could result in less or more fasting than once a week. Whenever and however you choose to fast, my hope is that establishing this spiritual discipline in your own life will draw you closer to Jesus who (after fasting for 40 days) withstood the devil's temptations. - Steve Beard.

CHAPTER FOUR - THE TWELVE
From the Kitchen to the Living Room

"And he called to him his twelve disciples and gave them authority over unclean spirits, to cast them out, and to heal every disease and every affliction.² The names of the twelve apostles are these: first, Simon, who is called Peter, and Andrew his brother; James the son of Zebedee, and John his brother;³ Philip and Bartholomew; Thomas and Matthew the tax collector; James the son of Alphaeus, and Thaddaeus;[a] ⁴ Simon the Zealot,[b] and Judas Iscariot, who betrayed him" - Matthew 10:1-3 (ESV).

¹³ And he went up on the mountain and called to him those whom he desired, and they came to him. ¹⁴ And he appointed twelve (whom he also named apostles) so that they might be with him and he might send them out to preach¹⁵ and have authority to cast out demons. ¹⁶ He appointed the twelve: Simon (to whom he gave the name Peter); ¹⁷ James the son of Zebedee and John the brother of James (to whom he gave the name Boanerges, that is, Sons of Thunder); ¹⁸ Andrew, and Philip, and Bartholomew, and Matthew, and Thomas, and James the son of Alphaeus, and Thaddaeus, and Simon the Zealot, [b] ¹⁹ and Judas Iscariot, who betrayed him. - Mark 3:13-19 (ESV).

¹² In these days he went out to the mountain to pray, and all night he continued in prayer to God. ¹³ And when day came, he called his disciples and chose from them twelve, whom he named apostles: ¹⁴ Simon, whom he named Peter, and Andrew his brother, and James and John, and Philip, and Bartholomew, ¹⁵ and Matthew, and Thomas, and

James the son of Alphaeus, and Simon who was called the Zealot, [16] and Judas the son of James, and Judas Iscariot, who became a traitor. - Luke 6:12-16 (ESV)

It doesn't take long in reading the different accounts to first of all understand that we are faced with a difficulty. It appears that the lists of the 12 cannot always be unified or that they fit together. It at first appears that at different times, different individuals may have made up the inner 12.

And of course we cannot have that happen. So, we do some maneuvering to do our best to say that our writers are using other parts of their names, that Jesus came out with 12 Apostles and stayed with 12 Apostles.

But, what if for example, after following Jesus for a while one or two left or changed their minds, and Jesus picked another one or two? Did it happen? We really don't know. All we know is that these individuals, along with others like Mary, Martha, Lazarus, and others enjoyed what we are going to call the Relationship of the 12.

A relationship that takes us deeper than just the receiving and feeding crowd. A relationship that takes us even deeper than the serving and partnering crowd. We would be amiss if we only looked at this "12" as only 12, as if the number 12 signified just 12 people. When in fact, what we should look at is the relation this 12 had with Jesus. As we look at that, we also see that others had a very similar relationship with Jesus.

A relationship that can be labeled as "follower". People who are willing to follow Jesus at any cost. People who take up Jesus' mission to be intimate, that choose to be humble, that choose to be loyal and that choose to walk in the steps of Jesus.

How does this group differ from the seventy? Not by much. Both groups did and saw amazing things. But Jesus calls us to be more than workers. He calls us to be followers.

Perhaps an example here would help us. There is no finer example of one traveling the road of being a part of the 70, a part of partnering and serving to being a true follower than in the tale of two sisters, Mary and Martha. For in this story we see the adventure of the transformation of a doer to one who is becoming, from a servant to a true follower of Jesus. A follower ready and willing to put all to the side to sit at His feet, to become the disciple who can then do more than ever for the Kingdom in Christ Jesus.

We find their story in Luke 10:38-42. Jesus had been traveling and doing all kinds of stuff. He had been teaching and preaching. He had been casting out demons and freeing people of all kinds of illness and sickness. He had been hearing and rejoicing in the report of the 72, who themselves were able to teach and preach and heal and free people from demonic possession and oppression.

These were great days in Jesus' ministry and for those that had been a part of His life. Luke tells us that as they were traveling one day they all came to the house of Lazarus where he lives, along with his two sisters, Mary and Martha.

The trio invited Jesus and all of His disciples in, along no doubt, with a host of others. So, as they all pile in to hear Jesus teach and preach, we see two drastic differences between the two sisters. Mary leaves everything and goes and sits at Jesus' feet.

Martha, on the other hand, headed to the kitchen to prepare a meal. Martha began to do all she could to serve the needs of all those in the other room. They were hungry and she knew in her heart she could take care of their needs. No doubt that gave her great comfort. For one of the greatest joys of following Jesus is to be able to serve others.

The 72 had returned rejoicing because they had been able to serve others. They had done more than just "receive and feed." They had been involved in life changing events.

So it was with Martha. She was doing her best to meet the needs of others. However, that is not what Jesus seeks most in our relationship with Him. At this moment, He wants all the Marthas of the world, all the doers, and all those that love to serve, to come and sit at His feet and be followers.

Now, we have to understand that what Martha was doing was not wrong. It was not wrong for her to serve. It was not wrong for her to want to take care of the needs of others. However, at this moment Jesus was inviting her to a deeper relationship – that of being a true follower. One that would give Jesus her heart. People who would leave what they were doing to just be in Jesus' presence.

When Jesus told His other followers to follow Him, He wanted them to put down what they were doing and give Him their full attention. To be still and know. To be still and learn. To be still and watch. To be still and experience. To be still. Quiet. Repose. At peace.

We are called to serve. We are called to be active. But, we are more called to follow in Jesus' footsteps. We are called more to be in His presence. We are called to follow Jesus in doing His plan. We are called to simply do whatever is necessary to follow Him closer. We are called to put aside anything and everything to follow Him.

Does that mean we go from "serving and partnering" to once again "receiving and feeding"? I mean, it appears that Martha has transition to be a member of the "72," while little 'ole Mary is slide back in the "5,000" - just sitting there just absorbing and getting fed and not worrying about how she can serve.

On the surface it does look that way. It looks like Martha is the righteous one. After all, she is doing her best to serve all those under the roof of their house. But, as we truly hear the words of Jesus we come to a much deeper understanding of what true service involves.

Jesus' primary mission in coming to their house that day was not to be served a meal. There would be plenty of time for everyone to sit down and share a meal. Right now, the main thing that Jesus was desiring was for His followers to simply rest in His presence. Right now, the main thing Jesus wanted all his disciples to understand was that before one partakes of physical food it is vital that one partakes of spiritual food.

Jesus had not asked to be fed. Jesus had not come to the house to get a meal right then. Jesus had come to pour out His life into their lives. Jesus had come so that they could follow Him.

So much of Martha was wrapped up into that kitchen of hers. It was there she could shine. It was there that she could serve. It was in service that she found her identity. But Jesus was calling for her, and for us, to find our true identity in Him. Jesus does not want to forget about serving. Jesus loves for us to put our faith into action. However, Jesus wants us to go in the strength and power of the LORD. And that can only happen if we spend time in His presence, at His feet, listen and resting in Him.

For as we grow closer to the LORD and especially as we find out we can partner with Jesus, we tend to become little robots. We become people who learn what they can do for the LORD and spend more time in the doing for Jesus than being with Jesus.

This is what happened to Martha. She traded a life of being in Jesus for a life of doing for Jesus – not of itself a bad thing. But, we are called to a life of being in Jesus rather than just doing things for Jesus. When we continually do things just for Jesus we tend to lose our ability to serve with joy and gladness.

Martha did. She got caught up so much in wanting to do something for Jesus that she allow her anger to get the best of her and she interrupts Jesus and asks Him to correct this sister of hers. She demands Jesus to tell Mary to get with it, to get into the kitchen and start doing things instead of just being with Jesus and in Jesus.

Here she was, wanting so much to do something for Jesus that she ended up trying to tell Jesus what to do. She went from being that of a servant to that of a boss. In no time flat, she interrupted Jesus and demanded that He meet her needs – right now! In no uncertain terms, she said to Him, to tell Mary 'to get her little self off the floor and come in the kitchen and start serving. How dare she sit at Your feet LORD, following You, and listening to You. Send her back into the thick of things. There are biscuits to be made, lamb to cook, and honey to be put into the cups. There is wine to pour and all You are doing is allowing her to sit and listen, to sit and follow You.'

The call to follow Jesus is a call to intimacy. It is a call to humility. It is a call to forget about yourself (Matthew 16:24). It is a call to holiness and a call allow Jesus to set the agenda.

Again, what Martha was doing was not wrong, it was simply not the best. Service is a wonderful relationship to have with Jesus. Millions of Christians around the world enjoy this depth of relationship. Jesus desires us to experience more. He desires us to experience Him. He desires for us to put Him first and everything else second, even if that everything else involves taking care of the needs of others.

In our world today there is a great need for the Social Gospel. More than ever we need to speak out against things like human trafficking, income inequality, social injustice, racial divide, gender inequality, domestic abuse, and a host of other issues. We need to be the Church in Action. We need to be the Church in the soup kitchens, in the rehab centers, and in the homeless shelters. We need to be participants in the marches against social evils of all kinds.

But, we also must do them in Jesus and not for Jesus. We must not just make bread for Jesus. We must partake of the Bread called Jesus. In other words, we must take the time to be saturated by His Presence and not just attempt to do things to promote His cause.

If we don't, we will quit. If we don't sit as His feet, if we don't take this next step of following Him with all our hearts and lives, then we find ourselves more often than not, frustrated, ready to quit and fussing with Jesus – even to the point we attempt to tell Jesus what to do.

This time Mary had it going on. Later we see she has some issues to deal with after her brother died. As you read that story, (John 11:17-44) you see that Martha's faith has grown where Mary is suffering from the effects of grief at the time. Neither one does anything wrong. It's just that here is where Mary shines, later we see Martha shining.

We can shine as we decide that it is more important to follow Jesus than to just serve Him. We can do both, but it needs to be done in the right order. We serve to follow Him and in following Him we better understand and are able to serve in Him.

It is a subtle thing this serving for Jesus and then serving in Jesus. This invitation of making sure everything is second to Jesus. It is a vital thing. It is the very thing that can cause us to rejoice in our walk with the LORD or to become a spiritual complainer, a spiritual busybody, a spiritual score card master and judge.

Joanna Weaver in her excellent little book, <u>Having a Mary Heart in a Martha World</u>, (on page 9), calls it on page 9 "possessing a Martha's kitchen or a Mary's Living Room Intimacy." The difference is between knowing Jesus and serving Jesus. Performing for Jesus or knowing Him intimately as LORD. While the world, and even the church at times, calls us to do more and more, the Father whispers for us to "Be still and know."

Martha suffers from being distracted to being discouraged, to becoming demanding. We will experience the same. We must take time to sit at His feet, to become single minded, to become saturated in Jesus and then to be able to serve and soar with joy.

It is easy to get lost in doing things for Jesus. After all, there is great joy in doing things for others. There is great joy in being that one that can feed and take care of others. But, in doing so we must make sure that we don't disconnect ourselves from the sources of life. Just as it is important for the branches to produce fruit (works, service, partnership), it is vital that they stay connected to the vine (to sit at Jesus' feet).

How is it with you? Have you found yourself in the shoes of Martha? Wanting to be more than just "watching and listening", more than just "receiving and feeding". You want to do something for Jesus. You want to be a part of His team. You want to get your hands dirty and do something to promote the Kingdom of God. Good for you! We need more like you. We need more to accept a relationship with Jesus that will move their hands and their feet that will cause them to work in soup kitchens, and teach small groups and lead in prayer services.

We also need to make sure that we take the next step of not just doing, but being. Being a follower of Jesus. That means that when Jesus is in the room, He takes our full attention. He leads. He is in command. If He says to make bread, then that is what we do. If He tells us to get active then active we become active. But, when He teaches, we sit down at His feet. When His Word is read, we become quiet and listen. When His Spirit whispers we make sure that we are still enough to hear and obey.

I love the fact that as you read all of Martha's story she undergoes a "holy makeover" (Joanna Weaver's words on page 151 of her book). A holy makeover in which she experiences Jesus a whole new way, a whole new relationship with Jesus. The relationship of being a true follower, not just a doer.

Doing without becoming will lead us down a path of distraction, diversions, doubt, demands and destruction. We will find ourselves trying to tell even Jesus what to do and how to do it.

The only way we can serve with joy is to focus on becoming more of a follower of Jesus than a doer of Jesus. For the deeper we follow Jesus we soon discover the reality is that we can do more in Jesus than we can do for Jesus. Why all the concern? Why even deal with the Martha issue? Because of what we see in Judas. He too started off wanting more and more, to experience more than just listening and feeding. He, however did not ultimately want Jesus. He wanted to serve Him, but when that service demanded him to go a different direction, Judas decided to cash it all in.

As intimate as a relationship of the 12 can be, we must continue to sit at the feet of Jesus. We must continue to be more like Jesus or else we will turn around and betray this One that we first claimed to love.

Benedict Arnold was on the inside of the American army and betrayed his troops. Brutus made himself famous for betraying his king and friend. Brutus was considered to be the closest of friends to Julius Caesar right up to the time he stabbed Caesar with a dagger.

Judas denied Jesus with a kiss. A kiss of one who was supposed to follow Him. One who was a part of the "12". He started his walk away from Jesus by trying to make sure his service was profitable for himself. He started walking away by again listening to the crowds. He started walking away until he found himself no longer knowing what was important.

You see, you can be physically close to Jesus but be miles away in your heart, your mind, and your soul. Even though each day for years

Judas walk in the dust of Jesus, at some point he did not allow Jesus to stay in his heart and life. Judas followed Him for a while, but he turned away. He listen, he watched, he received, he feed, he even served (no doubt he was at first a part of the 72), he followed for a while; but, in the end he left the living room of intimacy, the kitchen of service, and went back to his den of selfishness and greed.

The same Devil that lured him back is constantly at work trying to lure us back. Hell has no greater joy than to watch one who has followed turn back and become a betrayer. The saddest words written about Judas we find in Mark 14:21 - *"It would be better for him if he had not been born."*

Now, does that mean that the LORD never wanted Judas to be born? Of course not. It does mean that it would have been better for him never to have existed than for him to have, in the end, not followed Jesus. For what is true of Judas is also true of you and me. Let us recommit our lives to Him, to Jesus right now. Let us take again the words of Oswald Chambers and live a life in which "conscious repentance leads to unconscious holiness".

Let us pray:

Dear Heavenly Father,

Praise Your Holy Name!   Praise to the LORD Almighty, Maker of all that exists in heaven and on earth.   It is in You, O LORD that we find our purpose and in You we put our trust.   In You, O Lord we have received Salvation, Redemption, and Holiness.   You have graciously pour out upon us, Your forgiveness, Your mercy and Your righteousness. Lead us to a deeper walk, to a deeper relationship with You, Jesus. Open our hearts and minds to show us Your Way. Lead us to follow Your paths, O Lord. Sweet Holy Spirit, guide us, lead us and teach us. We want to follow only You.

Jesus, we love to serve You. We love the joy and the celebration we experience when we serve others for You. We love to partner with You in bringing about healing and holiness into the lives of others. But we realize we are being called to an even deeper walk with You. A deeper walk that while it still involves service, it is one that takes us from our kitchens of service to the living room of intimacy. To the place where like Mary, we sit at Your feet. A walk that enables us to live in You, not just for You. A relationship and an experience that will lead us to be more than just doers. We desire to know more fully what it means to BE in Your Spirit. To be more than to do. To be more one with You than ever before. This is our plea, this is our prayer. We pray this in Jesus' Name. Amen.

Now let's turn to the fourth spiritual discipline. One that will help our hearts and our souls enjoy even more the presence and peace of Jesus. Turn the page.

SPIRITUAL DISCIPLINE #4
The Discipline of Solitude

If fasting today is seen as something that does not fit in with our culture of eat, eat, eat, then the discipline of solitude has to also be seen as something quite alien in nature. And it is; at least, for us living the 21st century. For we equate solitude with loneliness, and yet it is everything but loneliness. Loneliness brings heartache and despair. Loneliness brings us into a state of emptiness.

Solitude is the exact opposite. It is in our times of solitude that we find true inner contentment. It is in our times of quietness and solitude that we find a peace that passes all understanding. Solitude enables us to be more connected. It enables us to be more involved in life in meaning and fulfilling ways.

For Jesus calls us from our loneliness to places of solitude. From loneliness? Surely, we who live in the 21st century do not suffer from loneliness! I mean, all around us is human noise. We exist in a world of hash tags, Facebook, Instagram, and a multitude of other ways to communicate and connect. And yet, for all of our media, we are a planet filled with loneliness. The 21st century has been to be labeled the digital age, the age of information. Sadly, more and more it is also being labeled as the Age of Loneliness.

We fear being alone. Total silence brings on anxiety attacks. The sound of solitude petrifies us. Our fear of being alone drives us into a world of noise and crowds. We attempt to keep up a barrage of tweets,

Facebook message and Instagram, all in the hope that somehow they will bring deeper meaning in our lives. Yet, in the middle of all that human noise we feel more alone than ever. For in reality it is not noise that we seek, it is true connection. It is true relationship. It is true meaning in our lives. And, it is through the discipline of solitude that we can find balance. It is through solitude that we can regain ways to be with one another.

So, exactly what is solitude? Basically, it is getting away from all forms of distractions in our lives and spending some quality time in the Presence of the LORD.

There is no better example of the discipline of solitude than we see in the life of Jesus. We see that Jesus lived a life of "inward solitude." He took time away from the crowds to not just be alone, but to be alone with His Heavenly Father. Solitude in the Christian Life is not going somewhere and experiencing a state of nirvana. It is not a time of emptying oneself to nothingness. It is going to a place where one can hear God. Where all of one's senses can be attuned to best hear God as He reaches out to touch us, to speak to us, to lead and guide us.

It is not by accident that before Jesus went into full time ministry He spent some "solitude" time with His Father. When Jesus needed to absorb the death of His cousin John, we see Him doing the same thing. After the great miracle of feeding the 5,000 where do we find Jesus but going up on the mountain for a time of solitude. Jesus takes some time to get away from all the human noise to spend time with the Father in quietness, in solitude.

The great Henri Nouwen teaches us the importance of solitude, "without solitude it is virtually impossible to lead a spiritual life." Why does he say that? Because, it is in our times of solitude, in our times of being alone and still before the LORD that we are able to best hear God. It is during those times that we are best able to be transformed. It is in our times of solitude that discover how best to be both with the LORD and with others.

But isn't it quite selfish for us to take the time to be by ourselves? I mean aren't the needs of the world so great that we don't have the time to get alone? And with all that is going on around me, how do I take the time? Surely, this is one of those optional spiritual disciplines. Go back a couple of paragraphs and reread. Jesus needed His solitude, His alone time with the Father to accomplish His mission. So, too do we. We need our time for solitude.

Not everyone will understand our need for some quiet time. Even our families and closest friends may not comprehend this time that we need to set aside to be with the LORD. They may even think that we are trying to be some kind of super Christian, when in reality we only want to be more like Jesus. The same Jesus, who as we have seen, took time out to be with the Father.

We may even hear the hiss of the snake that tells us that it will be a waste of time. Precious time that could be used to serve others. In reality, our "Jesus alone" time, our time that we set aside to be in solitude to the Lord of our souls will be our best time. It will not only strengthen our soul it will give us a renewed energy to do all the mission that the LORD has for all of us.

Richard Foster rightly talks about solitude as a time of a second, third, fourth and fifth.... conversion. What he means by that is not that we have fallen from grace and have to experience a time of renewal time and time again. It is during our times of solitude with the LORD that we turn from the idols of the marketplace to the glory of God in the face of Jesus. As Foster writes, "God takes this 'useless" Discipline, this 'wasted time,' to make us His friend." (page 45 of Richard Foster's Study Guide for Celebration of Discipline).

Solitude is not so much about silence as it is about listening. Solitude is not so much about our getting away from all the noise of life, but getting in tune with the voice of God. We are not to take our alone time, our solitude with God, as a time to simply experience silence. Although, times of silence in and of themselves are helpful. We all need times of just quietness, of stillness.

Solitude is not so much passive as it is active. Solitude is a set time that we construct so as to hear, to see and experience more of God than ever before in our lives.

So, what is the difference between prayer and solitude? They can very much be the same and yet, the goal of true solitude is to in repose, to be in God's rest. It is that time that we set aside just to be in His

Presence. It is that time that we learn how to be still, how to quieten the heart and the tongue. It is that time that we allow the LORD to begin to teach us how to talk and how to communicate with Him and others. Sometimes while that can be done with words, many times it can be done best without words. There is time to talk and there is a time to not talk.

As a young man it use to cause me some anxiety to go home and visit my parents. It seemed like they could sit in the same room and not talk to each other. At the time I too was married and it seemed like in our marriage that there was never any time for silence, My wife and I had so much to learn about one another, so much to share. We were constantly chattering away. For a great while I thought what had happened was that mom and dad just had talked themselves out over the years, that they were tired of each other, that they simply had nothing to say to one another. I thought it was sad what had happened to them.

And now, some 30 years later, I find myself experiencing the same kind of relationship. But, what I have learned is that they did not run out of things to say. They were not tired of each other. Just the opposite. Instead, they had gotten so comfortable, so close to one another that they did not always need to fill the air with words. What I had failed to notice was the gentle glance across the room. The brush of a loving touch as one would go by the other. What I had failed to notice was that they had grown deeper in their love for one another, deeper than words.

What I had failed to see that was in their silence their togetherness was growing deeper and deeper.

Proverbs 25:11 tells us, *"A word fitly spoken is like apples of gold in a setting of silver."* And *"Be not rash with your mouth, nor let your heart be hasty to utter a word before God, for God is in heaven, and you upon earth; therefore let your words be few."* (Eccl. 5:2).

In is from our times of solitude that we learn better how to speak and even when to speak. For when we come before the LORD to listen, to hear, we suddenly no longer feel the need to control the world around us. No longer is there a need to straighten others out, including ourselves. Solitude allows us to rest in the LORD. It allows us to be in liberty with the LORD. It allows us to rest and be healed in His Presence.

So, how then do we practice the discipline of solitude?

1.   The first thing we can do is to take advantage of the "little solitudes" that fill our day. There are those little periods of time that we find ourselves alone and quiet. It may be that time when we have our morning cup of coffee or when we are traveling alone in our cars to work. It might be that time when we are alone at work eating in our cubicle. It may be even that time when we are waiting for the fish to bite or the deer to walk up.

These little periods of time can be golden. Why not allow them to become time of quietness and stillness before the LORD? While they will not give us all the necessary time we need to be quiet before the

LORD, they can help us a great deal. We can use them to connect with the LORD so that for the rest of the day we enjoy a peace that does pass all understanding and we can experience a supernatural control over our speech. For more than anything, solitude helps us to learn how to speak when we need to and what to say when words are needed.

Solitude helps us to understand that we do not need to always justify ourselves, even when we have messed up. We ask the LORD and any other parties for forgiveness and then travel on. We confess, we repent, and we progress.

All too often we attempt to fix every situation with a plethora of words. We try to rationalize and justify our actions with many words. When more often than not, we are better off to just be still and quiet. Solitude enables us to allow our Heavenly Father to take control. Silence is ultimately related to trust. Silence and solitude causes us to become quiet so that the LORD can move in our behalf. And who better can forgive or promote our cause than our Heavenly Father?

2. Secondly, we can create a place of solitude in our lives. Perhaps it is a little section of our house or in our garage or patio. Perhaps it is a local park that we can simply go and walk. Wherever that place is, it is to be a place that we can retreat to and experience a time of rest and quiet before the LORD.

If we cannot build such a place, perhaps we can designate a time and place in our house. A chair or a room that for a period of time is dedicated to just being quiet before the LORD. Susanna Wesley, mother of both John and Charles Wesley not only had those two boys to deal with, but eight other children. Can your image the workload? Can you imagine all the noise of that many children? How in the world could a mother of 10 running around have time to be quiet before the LORD? Susanna had promised the LORD when she was young that she would always take time to be silent before Him. Of course, she had said that before her house was so full of children. And, with all the work to be done with 10 children in the mid-18th century one would have thought her promise to the LORD impossible. You and I might have encouraged her to give up such a notion considering it just a part of her being naïve, that she needed to be sensible and just realize that the LORD would understand her plight.

Susanna told her family, and taught them, that when her apron was over her head to understand that she was taking her time out to be with the LORD. So, each day a time was set aside when Susanna would take her apron and pull it over her head, creating a sacred space for her and the LORD. Her family learned that this was mom's time to be with the LORD.

It was through her discipline of silence and solitude that Susanna was able to find direction and peace, a peace that enabled her to pray for her children, to give the godly advice and to live a life of holiness. For Susanna, the question was never would I take the time to be with the LORD? The question was, how to I tell others that I must have the time? How do I teach my children that they too need their sacred time? So, mom's time became their time as well. By making sure she had times of solitude, she was in fact teaching and mentoring her children. It is little wonder that the LORD was able to use two of her sons, John and Charles to lead millions of people to Jesus and to give to the church more than 9,000 hymns and songs.

3. Thirdly, take up the discipline to make your words few and full. Now, this is difficult for most of us. Most of us love to communicate. But more often than not, we often are just filling the air with noise. Try to go an hour or two without talking. Extend that time to three or four hours, then move on to attempt an entire day. Don't do it as a law, but as an exercise, as an experiment to see how helpless at times we feel without words and how excessive we are dependent upon words, then to find new ways to relate to others.

4. Attempt to even expand that time. Go on a personal retreat of solitude. Use that time to communicate with the LORD. Use that time to allow God for a time of reorientation of your life. Use that time to be away from all the noises of life and spend some quiet time before the LORD. I personally have found those time to be ones that enable me to better hear the LORD's leadings and times of great spiritual renewal.

Like our Savior we all need to take opportunities to get away so that we can truly be present when we are with people, to be renewed in God's Spirit that we can be the person God calls us to be. Richard Foster points out that one of the true fruits of solitude is "increased sensitivity and compassion for others." (page 95, *Celebration of Discipline*). He then goes on to quote Thomas Merton as he observed:

"It is in deep solitude that I find the gentleness with which I can truly love my brothers. The more solitary I am the more affection I have for them. It is pure affection and filled with reverence for the solitude of others. Solitude and silence teach me to love my brothers for what they are, not for what they say." (Celebration of Discipline, page 95).

Is it easy in our age to get quiet? No, but there never existed a more desperate time for us to be still and silent before the LORD. For it is in times like these that we are in most need of brothers and sisters in Christ to practice times of solitude. Our world needs to hear the message of Jesus. It needs the Church to be as close as ever to its LORD. It needs us to be at our best, and that should encourage us and create within us a passion to be still and quiet before the LORD.

How about it? Don't begin to think why you can't take some time away. Instead, make it a part of your schedule. Make it a part of your daily, weekly, and monthly walk with the LORD. Circle the calendar. Tell others you need to go somewhere. Find a park to walk around. Go to a lake and spend some time in quietness before the LORD. Set your alarm clock once a week, or month, to spend an hour or two in quietness before the LORD. Create a space in your life where God can reach you. If you have to pull an apron over your head. Whatever it takes make some quiet time. We all need it, and we will all be the better for it.

CHAPTER FIVE - THE POWER OF THREE

And after six days, Jesus took with him Peter and James and John his brother, and led them up a high mountain by themselves. - Matthew 16:1 (ESV)

Then Jesus went with them to a place called Gethsemane, and he said to his disciples, 'Sit here, while I go over there and pray. And taking with him, Peter and the two sons of Zebedee, he began to be sorrowful and troubled. - Matthew 26:36-37 (ESV)

As for the resurrection of the dead, have you not read what was said to you by God. I am the God of Abraham, and the God of Isaac, and the God of Jacob? He is not the God of the dead, but of the living. - Matthew 22:31-33(ESV)

But Moses' hands grew weary, so they took a stone and put it under him, and he sat on it, while Aaron and Hur held up his hands, one on one side, and the other on the other side. So his hands were steady until the going down of the sun. - Exodus 16:12 (ESV)

When the Sabbath was past, Mary Magdalene and Mary the mother of James and Salome brought spices, so that they might go and anoint him." - Mark 16:1 (ESV)

And the word of the LORD came to me; 'Son of man, when a land sins against me by acting faithlessly, and I stretch out my hand against it and break its supply of bread and send famine upon it, and cut off from it man and beast, even if these three men, Noah, Daniel and Job, were in it, they would deliver but their own lives by their righteousness, declares the LORD God." - Ezekiel 14:12-14 (ESV)

Shadrach, Meshach, and Abednego answered and said to the king, 'O Nebuchadnezzar, we have no need to answer you in this matter. If this be so, our God whom we serve is able to deliver us from the burning fiery furnace, and he will deliver us out of your hand, O king. But if not, be it know to you, O king that we will not serve your gods or worship the golden image that you have set up. - Daniel 3:16-18 (ESV)

It appears God loves the number three. The number three, or its compounds, just happen to occur hundreds of times throughout Scripture. In fact, it appears some 467 times. Most of the "3's" mark the number in quantity whether in enumerating persons, things, or activities. For example, Noah had three sons (Gen 6:10) while we are told Job had three daughters (Job 1:2; cf. 42:13). Inside the Ark of the Covenant there were three sacred objects 'The gold jar of manna, Aaron's staff that had budded, and the stone tablets of the covenant" (Heb. 9:4) The young warrior David is said to have "bowed down before Jonathan three times, with his face to the ground" (1 Sam 20:41), while the old prophet Daniel regularly prayed three times a day, giving thanks to God (Dan 6:10, 13). Israelite men, once they got to a certain age, were required to appear before the Lord three times in a year: "Three times a year all your men must appear before the LORD your God at the place He will choose: at the Feast of Unleavened Bread, the Feast of Weeks and the Feast of Tabernacles" (Deut 16:16). Jesus answered Satan's threefold temptation by citing three scriptural passages Matt 4:1-11). Paul experienced three shipwrecks (2 Cor 11:28) and prayed three times to the Lord for the removal of his "thorn in the flesh" (2 Cor 12:7-8). And of course, we are baptized in the name of the Father, the Son and the Holy Spirit (Matthew 28:19).

But the "three" gain even more importance when it comes to looking at human relationship, with one another and most importantly in relationship with the LORD. The above Scriptures point out some of the most famous trios - Abraham, Isaac, and Jacob. Noah, Job, and Daniel. Moses, Aaron, and Hur. Mary Magdalene, Mary, and Salome.

And no greater trio existent than that of Peter, James, and John. No relationship ever existed like that we see in Scripture between Peter, James, and John with Jesus. For as we examine this trio's relationship with Jesus, we find ourselves being invited to go even deeper in our relationship with Jesus. A relationship of faith, of deep prayer, and a relationship of both victory and suffering.

Let's take a moment and review and reflect our journey so far. Remember the statement made by pastor and author J. Oswald Chambers, *"We are as close to God as we choose to be".* (Robert Crosby, THE ONE JESUS LOVES, page 11). That statement is our premise and our challenge to do all we can to be close to the LORD. In the previous chapters we have studied and examined different depth levels of relationships that can exist between us and the LORD. Relationships that we have labeled as:

    + The Overall Crowd of Humanity based on Romans 1 - All humans that have ever been or will be born, all those that make up the world in which Jesus came to give everlasting life. All those who Jesus came to bring forgiveness, mercy and grace.

+ The Inner Crowds - those multitudes that came out of the "world crowd" and went to watch and listen to Jesus. *This is where many of us started.* This is where many of us started because we felt a pull towards Jesus. There was something about Jesus as we watched and as we heard His words that drew ever closer to Him.

We did not know it then, but that "it" was in fact the HOLY SPIRIT leading us and guiding us to come to Jesus. He was the one who first drew us to listen and watch Jesus. It is by the hearing of His Word that we begin our road towards salvation.

+ The 5,000 - Includes those that wanted more than just watching and listening. There was something about Jesus that they knew in Him their needs would be meet, and sure enough they were. Jesus brought healing and Jesus met all their needs. They followed Him and became a part of the "receiving and feeding" fellowship. They knew in their hearts that Jesus had the answers.

As joyfully as it to know so many make it to this level, there is also a sadness. So, often this is where a majority of people stay. They stay in this "receiving and feeding" relationship. They ultimately only seek the Jesus that can always meet their need that they can always get something from. You hear them talking about having to change church locations because it is not meeting their needs are not being met, they are not being feed.

Jesus desires for us to have a deeper relationship than this "receive and feed." He seeks for us to allow Him to be our Bread of Life and our Living Water. He desires for us to experience Him more for His miracles and wonders, but to put Him as our LORD. To have our lives centered in Him not in our wants and needs.

+ The 72 - Includes those that wanted a relationship deeper than "receiving and feeding". The "72" include those that seek relationship in which they are partners with God in serving the needs of others. They enjoyed the relationship with Jesus that brought healing and wholeness into the lives of others. They rejoice in being able to pour out their lives into the lives of others.
They live and work in the kitchens of service.

+ The 12 - Include all those that have accepted Jesus' invitation to come even more into His Presence. To journey from the kitchens of service to the living rooms of intimacy. It includes those that are determined not to just do things for Jesus, but to live a life in Jesus. To be more than just a doer – to be in Christ. It includes those that will follow Jesus. Those know that the true leader in their lives is Jesus, and that the true nature of a disciple is that of allowing Him to lead, and for us to follow. Come and See becomes Come Follow Me.

Now, we come to the relationship circle of the "3". As we have seen, there are many trios, but we want to look at Jesus' inner three, made up of Peter, James and John. We want to look at some snapshots from their lives as witnessed in the Gospels. We want to witness their dogged determination to have a deeper faith in Jesus than perhaps they could have ever known. It was their desire not only to watch, listen, receive, feed, serve, sit, and follow, these men wanted to scale great spiritual heights with Jesus. They wanted to dig deep, and as we shall see, they were called to do both, to both climb, and to dig deep.

Jesus recognized their desire and so as always, He reaches out to all those that want to draw closer to Him. As usual, we see Jesus putting them through a test. In their case we see a book end of tests. At the beginning we see where Jesus invites them to a mountain of glory and at the end to kneel beside Him in a garden of immense pain, sorrow and grief. Jesus leads the three up the rocky climb of Mount of Hermon and across the lush grass and olive trees of the Garden of Gethsemane.

Both the mountain and the garden involved struggles. With the first, it is Jesus inviting the three to join Him to a prayer meeting some 9,400 feet in the air, up to the very top of Mt. Hermon. While Mt. Tabor has been seen the traditional site of the Mount of Transfiguration more evidence, thanks to scholars like R. H. Fuller and J. Lightfoot, now points us to Mt. Hermon. Mt. Hermon sits on northern border of modern day Israel and Syria.

It takes a climb of 9,400 feet to make it to the top. While it's not the tallest mountain the world, in that day 9,400 was a very difficult and scary climb. Jesus and the three made the climb without modern day back packs, hiking boots and protein bars. These men did it in robes and sandals and pure determination.

Jesus led these men up on that mountain top to do only one thing - pray. Pause on that a second. They did not go up to see the heights or to build a temple (although that was Peter's later suggestion). They went up to fall down on their knees and pray. They didn't even go all the way to make a sacrifice. They went there to sacrifice themselves on altars of prayer.

I am sure that when Jesus first gave the invitation for this mountain trip, it was most likely given to all of the 12 and perhaps even more. However, only three signed up. And those three probably did not have the slightest idea what they were getting themselves into that day. After all, they were simple fishermen. They were more adapted to living some 400 feet below sea level around the area of Galilee, not walking up pathways and rocks to ascend to the top of Mt. Hermon. These were not mountain men. They were used to sand, and beaches and the smell of fish.

If that was where Jesus was going to go, then they were going to go be with Him. They had decided in their hearts that they would follow Jesus anywhere and everywhere He chose to walk. That is one of the major keys to having a relationship with Jesus like the three. Wherever He invites us we have to already have made up our mind to go. We don't ask Jesus for directions, we simply walk in His dust. We simply follow the paths that His sandals are traveling.

What a trip this journey up the mountain must have been! No doubt it took a number of days going up and coming down. While it is true that there were a number of temples located all along the mountain path, the trails to get to them are not easy. To scale the mountain required great determination and no doubt more than enough bruised knees, skinned elbows, and stubbed toes. It involved having to regulate one's breathing as going up the air would be a little thin. It also involved experiencing sore muscles, some burning calves, and tired feet.

Again, why were they going to that mountain? Oh, I remember --- to be with Moses and Elijah. But did they know that? Not at first they did not. If Jesus had told all the others that if they went up on the mountain they would be able to see both Moses and Elijah, then He would have either been labeled to be even crazier than some already thought or he would have been the leader of multitude of folks trying their best to get up that mountain. I mean, if we could see Moses and Elijah we would all do our best to get on the top of that mountain even if we had to do it in robes and sandals. We would be pushing and shoving to get to the top the fastest, to be the first ones to see Moses and Elijah, to witness Jesus in all His glory.

But that was not the invitation. Of course, we know that is what happened, but that was not a part of the original invitation. The original invitation was that of a prayer meeting. Like some of the other threes -- like Moses, Aaron and Hur, like Meshach, Shadrach and Abednego, this trio of three first started off with a prayer meeting. Where Moses' trio saw glory in the victory on the battlefield, where Meshach's trio witnessed firsthand glory and victory in the fire, this trio saw Jesus in all His glory. They were able to get a small peek into what the real Jesus, the real Son of God looked like in all His glory. They had a little bit of heaven rolled back and they heard the voice of God the Father Himself.

  For you see, that is a part of what being determined to be closer to Jesus involves. It involves going with Jesus to a place of prayer. It involves us changing our day to be with Him in prayer. Prayer brings us into a deeper Kingdom experience and prayer opens up to us a deeper walk with our LORD. Prayer is the source of all our strength. Prayer is the key God uses to invite us into seeing Him as we never have before.

  Quickly, now let's turn our attention to the Garden of Gethsemane. As high and holy as the mountain top experience proved to be, Jesus had another trip for these three. Jesus knew that in order for them to experience a deeper walk with Him they would also need to join Him in this garden. This garden that, in some ways, was opposite from the mountain. For even though we see the glory of Jesus being displayed, it is a different aspect of His glory. It is the glory of suffering, for that too can be a glory.

  Once again, Jesus does not share with them what is going to happen. Once again, they are invited to another prayer meeting. For this one, they find themselves kneeling in the lush grass of an olive tree garden. Whereas you would think that between the two prayer meetings the one on the mountain would have involved the greatest amount of energy. It was just the opposite. The suffering that the disciples had to endure on the Mount of Transfiguration was physical. The suffering that they would have to endure in the Garden would be emotional and spiritual.

It look like an easy task. They were getting to walk through the cool of the Garden of Gethsemane, after a wonderful Passover Meal. All around them was lush grass. All around them was life. What a contrast from the rocks and thin air of the mountain. However, what they see and experience here is one of the deepest battle of all eternity. Jesus is dealing with the most difficult time of His life and He has invited His closest friends, the inner three to join Him. Jesus does not want to be alone. Not on the mountain nor in the garden. Especially not in the garden, no matter how cool the air was that evening, no matter how green the grass was, no matter all of the flowers and trees that are so full of life. For Jesus, it would be a garden pointing Him towards His upcoming trial, crucifixion and death. For Jesus, it would be one of the final reminders that very soon upon His shoulders would be placed the sins of all mankind.

It is easy to reflect and express how much we would have enjoyed that mountain trip. If only we could have been there, we would have done our best to have been the first at the top, to see Elijah and then Moses. To see Jesus in all His glory. And, to top it all off, hearing the very voice of God. Who doesn't want to sign up for that trip?

But, the garden. Now, that is quite another story. It's one thing to grab your sandals and head up the mountain, it's another thing to join Jesus as He sweats drops of blood. Peter, James and John are invited to be Jesus' prayer partner as He struggles with the knowledge that in just a few hours His whole life will change. Jesus will have to feel the kiss of betrayal and hear the curses of the crowds. Jesus will watch as the 5,000, the 72, the 12, and even the 3 fall away, leaving Him alone. He will feel His flesh rip apart with each fall of the lash as those around Him mock His name. In just a matter of hours, the same hands that He touched and brought healing will be fastened by nails to a cross. In utter shame and humility, He will be lifted high so that all those around can curse Him, mock, and ridicule Him. He will be labeled a traitor. He will be called a blasphemer. In just hours, Jesus will be the centerpiece of capital punishment, bookended by thieves.

He will be called to take upon the sins of all the world. He will be called to finish the mission that His father in Heaven sent Him to do. Jesus knew that it would come to this end. But knowing what will soon take place and actually going through with it, of course, is altogether different. So, we see Jesus reaching out to these three for companionship, for encouragement, and for prayer support.

This invitation to suffer alongside of Jesus is a part of drawing closer to Jesus. This is a vital part of being what Robert Crosby calls a confidant of Christ. We are called to share not only in Jesus victories but, also even more in His sufferings. We are called to choose to be alongside of Jesus in His passions, in His ups and downs, and His heights and depths. (Robert Crosby, THE ONE JESUS LOVES, page 205).

Just how close do we really want to be with Jesus? Will we follow Him up the mountain to have a time of prayer? Will we follow Him into the garden to have a time of prayer?

If we choose to follow Him into this relationship of "3" we will see heaven open and see miracles and wonders never before seen. However, at the same time will we have to accept the reality that our hearts will be broken into pieces by the struggles and challenges of sin and the world.

Jesus, through His Holy Spirit, left us both stories to read, to mediate over, and to digest. That is why we have the story of the Transfiguration and the story of the Garden in our Bibles. They are not just stories to read with our eyes, but with our hearts. We are to invite the HOLY SPIRIT to help us also climb that mountain, to feel the rocks and taste the air, to experience the wonder of His glory. We are to allow the HOLY SPIRIT to help us feel the dew of the grass as we kneel in the Garden, to experience the depth of sorrow and pain that Jesus felt that night.

Growing as Christ followers involves both the mountain and the garden. It requires us to become a part of the story. It involves us reading and meditating on His Word, to allow that Word to be more than mere words. To allow ourselves to become a part of His Story. To call upon the Holy Spirit to make it alive to us. For it to becomes a part of us.

Even though Paul was never a part of Jesus' inner three, the Apostle very well understand what it meant to both rejoice in the LORD and also endure suffering in the LORD. Perhaps even greater than these three, do we see this being fleshed out in the life of the Apostle Paul. So, we must understand that this relationship of the "3" does not begin and end with Peter, John, and James. They are merely examples that the HOLY SPIRIT has left behind for us to look at, examine and then emulate. They merely show us the way up the mountain and down to the garden. They merely point the way to grow deeper in the LORD.

I believe what Jesus wants for all of us is to experience the reality that our God is greater than we can ever hope to imagine. He knows that we will be overwhelmed at His glory and grace that is one of the things we can take from the mountain. Never had they seen such glory and never have we; but, like them, it is possible. Perhaps not in the same way in the same fashion; but, we can experience the glory of Jesus in our lives.

For we are invited to come into the fellowship of the "3". You and I are invited to go from being a follower to being one who is determined to stop for nothing to be close to Jesus, to tackle both the mountain and the garden.

And, as with them, it will come in our times of prayer. It will be in our prayer times that God will open up His glory. Like climbing up the mountain, it may not come all at once. It may take us some time of being with the LORD for Him to show us His glory. It will take us some time with Jesus to ascend to such heights.

I remember in my life it happened at the end of a three hour prayer session. I was alone at the church just spending some quiet time with the LORD. Pouring out my heart in prayers of adoration, confession, thanksgiving and supplication. I had not even planned for that long of a prayer time. It just happened on that day that the LORD would not allow me to leave His presence. One hour passed by and my heart was still hungering for something more. I knew that the LORD wanted me to experience a newness that day. I could feel it in my spirit, and so I waited and continued to pray. The second hour passed and still I was drawn to stay in prayer, and so I stayed. I stayed because I felt Him say to stay. We talked. Nothing grandiose. No great insights that I can remember. There was no set formula. Just God and me talking as we had done many times in the past.

And then, around the third hour all of sudden His glory fell. All of a sudden it seemed like God, Himself, stepped down from heaven and entered into the room. I was overwhelmed with His awesome and glorious presence. I could do nothing but enjoy Him. There was no talking, there was only Him filling the room with His Spirit. After just a few minutes, I remember telling Him that it was more than I could handle. There was more glory there than I could absorb. I could not handle any more of His Presence. It was more than I could have ever imagined or hoped.

I had waited three hours to receive Him and in less than fifteen I had experienced more than I could process, more than I could understand. It took me back. This was just a fraction of what John, Peter and

James saw and experienced that day on the mountain. This was what glory looked like, felt like. If I close my eyes, to this day I can still feel and experience some of the residue of that day. I can still feel the joy and peace that came in my life that day.

However, in a parallel fashion there has also been those moments like St. John of the Cross called "the dark night of the soul". Those times when all around you is darkness; not a darkness to harm you or to cause you punishment, but those times like Jesus where you find yourself in the garden, feeling all alone and hearing the words of a cross, of death beckoning you. Those times when your heart seems like it is going to break. You cry out to the LORD, plead, bargain, to do anything to stop it all. You hear nothing. You muster up the courage to even try harder, to plead even more, and still you find yourself in darkness, seemingly all alone. You find yourself beside Jesus, sweating and pleading and attempting to bargain. And like Your Savior, you come to the only answer that there is - Father, Your Will Be Done. You settle it. There is still a Calvary to experience, but no longer do you feel like you go in your own strength. There is Jesus, who has already paved the way and is there now, ready to go with you. There is that one named Jesus who has paid the ultimate price. A price that enables you and me to deal with our "little Gethsemanes and Calvarys" in the power and presence of His Holy Spirit.

Jesus invites all of us to experience this deepening relationship of faith, of being one that could be labeled a confidant of Jesus. A relationship that is determined to scale Rocky Mountains and kneel in lush gardens is not one that will suddenly cause us to become perfect. For as you go back and read, Peter has some difficulty on that mountain. He talked too much. He didn't know what to say. He didn't know how to be silent. Sometimes we are all like Peter.

Peter grew in faith that day but again, he is not perfect. Later as you know, he will find himself in deep waters, so deep that he almost drowns. He forgets at times. We forget at times that we must continually stay focused on Jesus. We all are on a progressive walk with the LORD in this life. One that is full of ups and downs.

James and John are not immune either. For they too talked too much, at times thinking too highly of themselves, and on occasion not be quite as loving as they need to be, wanting to go all "Elijah" on some poor Samaritans.

How deep do you want to go? How close to Jesus do you want to be? Are you ready to climb the mountain and walk across the garden? Are you ready to follow Him anywhere?

If you are, get in line. We have one more stop. The relationship of the One. We will look at the life of John, as he is only our example. For the life of the One, like the life of the "3", the life of the 72, the 5,000 and the inner crowd are open for all of us. Before we go into the relationship of the One, let's study another Spiritual Discipline. Let's look at the Spiritual disciple of simplicity.

SPIRITUAL DISCIPLINE #5
The Discipline of Simplicity

Simplicity is the opposite of duplicity. Where duplicity brings bondage, simplicity brings freedom. Where duplicity aligns itself with anxiety, simplicity aligns itself with peace.

Simplicity is the state or quality of being simple. Something which is easy to understand or explain is simple, in contrast to something complicated. Simplicity is the hallmark of a life of the disciple of Jesus.

According to St. Thomas Aquinas, God is infinitely simple. He is Almighty, but He is Simple. He is GOD. The Roman Catholic and Anglican religious orders of Franciscans have set a life of simplicity as their lifelong goal. They strive after simplicity. Members of the Religious Society of Friends (Quakers) practice what is called the Testimony of Simplicity, which is the simplifying of one's life in order to focus on things that are most important and disregard or avoid things that are least important.

It is with the Quakers practice in mind that we can best understand and practice the spiritual discipline of simplicity. We are to focus our lives to rid ourselves of as much complication as possible, to take as our motto the little Shaker hymn:

It's a gift to be simple,
It's a gift to be free,
It's a gift to come down where we ought to be,
And when we see ourselves in a way that's right,
We will live in a valley of love and delight!

When true simplicity is gained
To live and to love we will not be ashamed,
To turn and to turn will be our delight,
Till by turning, turning,
We turn 'round right.

    What does this mean practically? It means that we confront ourselves and ask ourselves some important questions. For example, questions for example like these:

1. Are we pretending to know more than we actually know?
2. Do we put on a mask when it comes to how we want others to see us?
3. Do we pretend to either be richer or even poorer than we are?
4. Do we want to impress people with our titles, our degrees, our honors?
5. Do we act our age or are we trying to be either younger or older?
6. Do we buy to impress?
7. Do we entertain to impress?

8. Can we take criticism without lashing out?
9. Do we tell our stories making sure we always appear in the best of lights?
10. Are we more fluff than true substance?

Living simple is just that. Letting our yes be 'yes' and our no be 'no'. It is resisting the lust for status and position and instead just accepting who the LORD has made us. It causes us to dress well but not over extravagant. It creates within us a modesty without feeling the need to have all eyes on us when we enter the room.

Simplicity causes us to adopt a lifestyle that both glorifies God for his gifts while at the same time glorifying God for ways that we can use a portion of those goods for others. It means that we do not always have to have the newest item, the newest car. Instead, we can decide to live a simple life and invest some of our resources into the lives of those less fortunate. We can take up Dr. Ronald J. Sider's spiritual economic philosophies in making sure that the 3 billion under paid fellow citizens on this planet find ways to provide adequately for their families. (His book, *Rich Christians in an Age of Hunger* is a great read). We can do that while at the same time enjoying the fruits that God has allowed us to reap, by simply choosing to live a more simple life.

For we live in a world in which we attempt to call covetousness by its pseudo name ambition.

We call hoarding "being prepared." We call greed, "industry." And we call being entitled, "American."

When in reality, they are what they are in the light of the Gospel. Much of our culture is sick. If we listen to every commercial, if we adopt every lifestyle portrayed on the internet, if we adopt a philosophy of this world, our lives will not be simple, they will be duplicitous. We will have to lie, steal, cheat, and put up false images to exist in such a world.

Jesus has a better life for us. A simple life. Richard Foster points out this life in his book, *Celebration of Discipline*. It can be lived out through 10 simple rules:

1. Buy things for their usefulness rather than their status.
2. Reject anything that is producing an addiction in you.
3. Develop a habit of giving things away.
4. Refuse to be propagandized by the custodians of modern gadgetry.
5. Learn to enjoy things without owning them.
6. Develop a deeper appreciation for Creation. Get close to the earth. Walk whenever you can.
7. Look with a healthy skepticism at all "buy now, pay later" schemes.
8. Obey Jesus' instructions about plain, honest speech.
9. Reject anything that will breed the oppression of others.
10. Shun whatever would distract you from your main goal.

In closing here are a couple of John Wesley quotes - a man who knew about how to live simple:

"Do you not know that God entrusted you with that money (all above what buys necessities for your families) to feed the hungry, to clothe the naked, to help the stranger, the widow, the fatherless; and, indeed, as far as it will go, to relieve the wants of all mankind? How can you, how dare you, defraud the Lord, by applying it to any other purpose?"
— *John Wesley*

"Do all the good you can. By all the means you can. In all the ways you can. In all the places you can. At all the times you can. To all the people you can. As long as ever you can." – *John Wesley*   Living a simple life will not always be easy nor will it be without controversy. As Dallas Willard so aptly writes in his book, *THE DIVINE CONSPIRACY*, we must be "prepared to be treated as more or less crazy". (page 213).

For to do and to live otherwise is to get caught in the trap of a life of anxiety. A life of worry. A life of frustration. More than one person has allowed things – possessions – materialism to capture and enslave them. We can be rid of such tangles by living a simple life.

Our Lord and Master Jesus had it right when He advised those who wanted to truly follow Him in Luke 10:1-12 to: Begin with prayer, saturate your life with prayer and end your life with prayer

Travel light - that is live simple

Live a life of peace

Believe that God will meet your needs

Know Your mission- that of healing, teaching, preaching, sharing

Rejoice in the victories.

CHAPTER SIX – INTIMACY:
THE CALL TO ONENESS WITH JESUS

One of his disciples, whom Jesus loved, was reclining at table close to Jesus ... - John 13:22 (ESV)

If you keep my commandments, you will abide in my love, just as I have kept my Father's commandments and abide in his love. These things I have spoken to you, that my joy may be in you, and that your joy may be full. - John 15:10-11 (ESV)

I do not ask for these only, but also for those who will believe in me through their word, that they may all be one, just as you, Father, are in me, and I in you, that they also may be in us, so that the world may believe that you have sent me. The glory that you have given me, I have given to them that they may be one even as we are one, I in them and you in me that they may know that you sent me and loved them even as you loved me. - John 17:20-24 (ESV)

Mary therefore took a pound of expensive ointment made from pure nard, and anointed the feet of Jesus and wipe her feet with her hair. The house was filled with the fragrance of the perfume ... - John 12:3-4 (ESV)

But the hour is coming, and is now here, when the true worshipers will worship the Father in spirit and truth, for the Father is seeking such a people to worship him. God is spirit and those who worship him must worship in spirit and truth. - John 4:23-24 (ESV)

There is little doubt that John the Apostle lived a very deep and intimate relationship with Jesus. John references himself as the "Disciple whom Jesus loved". John is present at the Transfiguration and the Garden of Gethsemane. John is the only one of the 12 that is present at Calvary. Jesus asks John to take care of Mary, His mother. It is John who runs to the tomb first and looks in and begins to realize that Jesus is alive, and it is John who was given the privilege years later to write the letter of Revelation. Many scholars down through history have commented on this intimate relationship that existed between the LORD and His young disciple, John.

Nevertheless, we would be amiss if we saw John as the "ONLY ONE". In fact, when one turns to John 11:3, one quickly sees that John is not the only disciple who was mentioned as the one whom Jesus loves. That title also was given to Lazarus, the brother of Mary and Martha. In sending the news about Lazarus, the sisters refer to him this way - "Lord, he whom you love is ill." (verse 3 ESV). The relationship John experienced and what John enjoyed with Jesus was not therefore exclusive to just John. John did not have a corner on the market of "oneness" with Jesus. In fact, as we look at his Gospel what we see is John inviting others to join his path. What we see in John's writing is an invitation to others to experience the same depth in relationship that he experienced, as well as Lazarus.

We all know from reading the Gospel of John that his writing is different from the others, from what we call the Synoptic Gospels (Matthew, Mark, and Luke). Matthew, Mark, and Luke seem to present us with a more historical account of the life of Jesus. They seem to write the story of Jesus as it was lived out over a three and half year period. John, however, appears to weave his story around different themes. He deals much more with interviews and conversations and does not seem to be bound to a certain historical time line. John is not so much concerned about when things happened but why they happened and what they mean in the larger context. John includes a great many more intimate details of Jesus' life and His encounters with various individuals.

I believe that in John's Gospel, he is sharing with us an invitation. An invitation to experience a relationship with Jesus at a depth that John was experiencing. I believe John wrote his Gospel with the intention of telling us the basic Story of Jesus, but also to invite us into a relationship of intimacy with Jesus. I believe John wants us to experience Jesus as he experienced Jesus.

It was not enough for John to share with us the simple life of Jesus. John wants to share so much more. He wants to tell us of the One who gives life from above. He wants to tell us of the one who is Living Water and who is the Bread of Life. John wants us to know who is the Way the Truth and the Life so that we too may experience Him. It John who wants us to know who is the Resurrection from the dead and who is Our Lord and Savior. John has this high Christology and He wants us to experience Jesus with our bodies, minds, and our spirits.

So, as you read John's Gospel, it is the story of telling us, showing us, and inviting us to be one with Jesus. John is inviting us to live a life far beyond that of simply watching and listening to Jesus, he wants us to move past a relationship based on receiving and feeding. John seeks for us to mature even beyond that of partnering and serving. John knows that there is an experience that is even deeper than us following in Jesus' footsteps. John wants us to enter into the Holy of Holies with Jesus. He wants us to experience the life of abiding, the life of intimate connection, the life of breathing in the Spirit (see John 15:1-17, John 17:1-26 and John 20:19-31).

John painstakingly leads us through all kinds of different encounters to show us these truths. He paints different scenes over and over, all with the intention of showing us what it means to be close to Jesus.

+ He shares with Nicodemus how he can be born from above, how through the Spirit, he can be born again and experience a oneness with Jesus. (John 3:1-21)

+ He shares how Jesus reaches out to the Samaritan at the well, in how Jesus can be Living Water. John shares the reality that Jesus is the Messiah, the One who saves us and redeems us. (John 4:1-45).

+He shares how Jesus reaches out to the wounded and hurting, one who, for 38 years, had been waiting only to have Jesus bring wholeness in their lives with a few words. (John 5:1-17).

+He shares how Gentiles like the centurion, just by their faith open the door towards intimacy and healing. (John 4:46-54).

+ He shares that Jesus will reach out to the sinner, even that one who is caught in the very act of sin. (John 8:1-11). Jesus invites that one also into a life of intimacy, forgiving sin and welcoming an intimate relationship in holiness.

In reading John's Gospel, you come to understand that there is no one outside of Jesus' invitation to this life, not even the man born blind (John 9:1-41). Only those who refuse to see, who refuse to accept Jesus as Lord, are those that will find themselves blind and lost.

Even disciples that boldly proclaim their allegiance only to end up warming themselves before fires of denial, (see John 18:25-27) are called again to Jesus; even they are welcomed back into a relationship of intimacy (see John 20:15-19). John takes great pains to paint picture after picture of what it means to start and continue a walk with Jesus.

How deep of a walk does Jesus desire for all of us? A walk so deep that takes us into a relationship of being "One In Jesus". It is this "oneness" that we see in the lives of John and Lazarus. And it is one that we see in Lazarus' sister, Mary. In John chapter 12 we find Mary sitting at Jesus' feet, soaking in His very presence. Officially, she was not a part of the 12 disciples, or a part of the inner 3, but as you read her story you realize that she shared an "oneness in Jesus" that was shared with John and Lazarus and others.

Let's turn to John 12 and share the story. Jesus has come for a visit. While it was not His first visit, it would prove to be His last visit.

Perhaps Mary sensed this fact. Maybe it was something she saw, something she heard Jesus say that told her that this visit was going to be different than any other that they had shared.

Perhaps as she met Him at the door she could see it in His eyes. For people who love each other can see and sense things that others are not able. Judas, for example, did not see anything.

To him, this was just another meal at Lazarus' house. He had no clue as to its importance.

John carefully lays out the story. At first, he only shares that Jesus came for a meal. Nothing more is alluded to or hinted. But sometime during the meal, Mary comes and sits at Jesus' feet. It was not the first time she had done so, but never had anyone done for Jesus what she was about to do. She sits at Jesus' feet and instead of seeking what she can receive from Jesus, she pours out her life on Jesus. She uncovers the deepest parts of her heart and pours them out upon the LORD. You may ask, now how did she do that? What did she do to make you think she was giving Jesus the deepest parts of her heart?

When Mary anointed Jesus at the banquet given in His honor, she was giving Him her very best. She first of all gave Him her future. For that is what the pound of nard was, it symbolized her future. Scholars tell us it probably was her dowry. Because no father is mentioned in any of the stories involving Lazarus, Martha or Mary, it has always been assumed that by this time that both of their parents had passed away, and that both girls were living in their brother's house for his protection.

That little bottle of perfume was worth over one year's worth of wages. Now, don't read that and just go on, bypassing its significance. Meditate on that little fact for a moment. Mull it over. Allow it to speak to you. One year's worth of wages. Take whatever you make in a year, and visible put it into a little container -- $15, 000, $25,000, $40,000, $60,000, $100,000 or more. Take that amount and place it over to the side. Even today with our ability to get anything we want around the world, a pound of nard (imported usually from India) goes for about $30,000.00.

During this time, tradition stated that when a woman and man married it was with the idea that for the first year they would not have to spend their time working hard, but would spend the majority of their time getting to know one another and adjusting to their lives together. That was the main reason for having a dowry and for all the wedding gifts that were given. It was to provide for the family a first start; and with that first start, giving them the opportunity to begin life, being able to spend more time together for the first year and not for just the first few days.

It makes one pause and wonder how many of our contemporary marriages might be saved if more money was invested that enabled the couple to spend more time with each other all year long instead of only the brief period of time we call a honeymoon. How much money is spent making sure that the first few days are shared, rather than the first year being blessed with less stress financially? Perhaps the people of Jesus' time were just a bit wiser than we are today.

Back to the dowry – without a dowry this whole one year of togetherness would be impossible, and to marry a woman without one would mean that the prospective groom would either have to be wealthy himself or would be forced to start the marriage out having to work hard each and every day. This one year of wedded bliss could either make or break a marriage.

So, the dowry was an extravagant gift that was to be given to the groom and therefore, to the couple. Mary, by all accounts, had by some means obtained one that was worth about a year's wages. After marriage, her and her husband would have sold it and used the proceeds to begin life together. Without a dowry, there was a good chance that she never would be married. In fact, tradition does not tell us that she did marry, for she would have entered into married life with very little to offer in the way of finances, and that to most young men was uninviting.

Mary not only gives to Jesus her future, she gives to Him, herself. For she begins to pour out her life as she anoints His feet. No doubt before she anoints them earlier, she had or else Jesus, Himself, had washed His own feet.

Nobody likes to wash feet. It's a messy, muddy, dirty job. We have already seen that even slaves could not be commanded to wash a person's feet – it was that disgusting of a job. It was a person's own responsibility to wash their own feet. It caused people to be careful where they stepped and what they stepped in going down the road. So, either Jesus had already washed His feet or Mary had done it for Him before she poured the nard. If in fact, the latter was true, then Mary has even displayed more of her love for Jesus.

It was upon these feet of her LORD, that we see Mary pouring out her life, her future. She is publicly proclaiming to everyone her intense love for Jesus. She knows that Jesus will not and cannot marry. She knows that is not a part of His divine plan. She understands that Jesus is the Messiah that He is the Son of God, and I believe she understands more than anyone else in the room that death laid in His future.

It is with that knowledge, and with that depth of love, that she pours out upon His feet this pound of nard. She begins to work it into His feet, taking the time to caress them, and then she does something even more intimate and strange, at least to us. She lets down her hair, the symbol of her glory, and she wipes the feet of Jesus with her hair. The room is filled with the smell of nard. The room is filled with the sacrifice of Mary, giving all of herself to Jesus.

For upon Jesus, Mary pours out her heart, her future, herself, and her glory. She holds nothing back. She is the living example of the depth one will go to be One with Jesus. She knows that they cannot marry and that is not a part of her sacrifice. But she knows that she can enter into a relationship that goes deeper than marriage. A relationship that John would later share with us in John 17 - to be One with the Father and with The Son. A Oneness that stretches back over all time and even before time. A Oneness that involves more than the physical but the inner most parts of the Spirit. It is the same reason why Jesus shared with the woman at the well the fact that true worship comes through the melting of spirits, our spirit with God's Spirit.

At the same time we see this living portrayal of what it means to be One with Jesus, we see all too clearly the exact opposite. We see through the actions of Judas a false love, a selfish love, a love that sought to only put oneself on the throne.

Judas even attempts to make his disdain of Mary's extravagant love look noble. He attempts to pawn off his love for the poor as the reason he can't display such love for and to Jesus; but, Jesus and others in the room know better. They had lived with Judas. They knew over the years his love had grown cold. They knew that Judas main love was for money, for power, for position and for his own self gain.

John calls him a thief. John tells us that Judas' love for himself outstripped any love that he had for Jesus. While John allows us this beautiful and supernatural love that existed between Mary and Jesus, he also give us this hellish look at how Judas chose himself and his own way. For Judas it was more about keeping riches than giving them over to Jesus. For Judas it was more about hiding behind a false mask of spirituality than it was being a living sacrifice at the feet of Jesus.

I wonder how long the smell of nard lasted both on Jesus and on Mary. I wonder in just a few days when Jesus was kneeling in the garden, if it wasn't still on the bottom of His robes. I wonder if it could still be floating around, reminding Him that He was loved by some of His disciples.

I wonder how long Mary waited before she attempted to wash the smell out of her hair, how long it lingered as the days went by. I am sure that others, like Judas, once hearing what she had done had questioned her actions that day. But, I am also sure that each time she looked at that alabaster jar, each time she smelled of its residue, she knew in her heart she had made the right choice.

Like the Wise Men before her, like Peter, James, and John, like Anna and Simeon, like the 120 later, Paul and Dorcas, and a billion later, she knew that she had made the right choice. She wanted to be as close to Jesus as possible. So, she gave Him her future, she gave herself to Jesus and she gave Him her glory.

What we see in Mary's story here in John 12, the Apostle goes on throughout the rest of his book to share with us. We see John, more than any other writer, giving us examples of how we too can find this intimacy with Jesus. All it takes is for us to:

1. Be willing to be a servant like Jesus - to give up our positions, our power, our minds, our bodies, and spirits and learn to wash feet.

2.	Be willing to be connected to Jesus as the branches are connected to the vine. A connection that brings life, a connection that involves allowing the Father to prune and cleanse.
A connection that in the end will produce life and even more life.

3. Be willing to be open to the Holy Spirit. Be willing to be convicted, to be guided, and to be brought into the very essence of the HOLY SPIRIT.

More than any of the other writers John spends a great deal of time sharing with us information about the presence and work of the Holy Spirit. He does so by design. This one who loved and was loved by Jesus, understood that power and presence of the Holy Spirit.

If you remember John was not known for his great love at the beginning. His nickname had nothing to do with love or loving. He was one of the original Sons of Thunder. It was more in John's nature to bring down fire upon those who appeared to not obey than it was to share with love, with the weak and wounded.

But, John was transformed. John shares with us Jesus' words of connection, of spirit in John 17. Either John was there, or by way of the Holy Spirit, these words were shared with John. Nonetheless, they point the way to Oneness. A Oneness that we are all invited to be a part of in our journey.

A Oneness that comes not so much by our actions, but by our willingness to surrender. A Oneness that comes not so much by our activity as by our opening up our hearts, minds and soul. A Oneness that while John experienced, it was not the first to experience it.

It was this Oneness that Adam and Eve enjoyed as God would come down in the cool of the day to walk with them. This Oneness in which there is this ability to be totally transparent, vulnerable and free. Free to be one's true self that is, a person made in the image of God Himself.

We lost that in the Garden. Instead we choose to mask ourselves, we choose to put ourselves before the LORD. We choose to be opaque rather than be transparent. We choose to be in control rather than to be vulnerable. We choose to be closed off, set apart for ourselves, rather than experience true freedom. For true freedom comes from openness. True freedom comes from being able to be one's true self, to be made and transformed into the image of Jesus. True freedom comes when we open our hearts, lives and minds to have them be renewed into the Image of Jesus. That takes more and involves more than you and I can do on our own. We cannot reform ourselves. If history has taught us anything, it is that we cannot change man for the best through human effort alone. There is no heaven on earth that can be made by the hands of men.

For as great of cultures as we have built over time, the reality remain, while some have had tinges of being heaven on earth, more often than not, each has fallen to more look like hell on earth. Each has gone the way of the sand and the dust of the air. Many have started well, but all have ended poorly.

It is beyond the scope of humanity to bring about this Oneness. But, it is the joy of the Holy Spirit to do so. For this is His most excellent work – to take the hearts and minds and bodies of men, women, boys and girls and lead them to a life of Oneness. To lead all through His cleansing, His redeeming Spirit and to join us bone-to-bone, marrow-to-marrow, mind-to-mind and spirit-to-spirit. To birth within us Himself, and through Himself, to lead us to experience a life with Jesus that goes beyond that of watching and listening, goes beyond that of receiving and feeding, that goes way beyond even partnering and serving, that goes beyond that of even following. It is a relationship of Oneness - of us being in the Spirit and the Spirit being in us. It is a rejoining of our Spirit, our bodies, and our minds with and in the Holy Spirit.

It is a Oneness that we see in Adam and Eve. It is a Oneness that is hinted at in the lives of those like Enoch, Noah, and Abraham. A Oneness that we see displayed in such lives as Joshua, Deborah, Ruth, Samuel, and David. A Oneness that we see in Elisha, in Isaiah, and in Jeremiah. A Oneness that we see in John, Peter, and James, along with Paul, Timothy, Dorcas, and Lydia.

It is a Oneness that we see throughout history in Polycarp, in St. Augustine, Luther, Calvin and Wesley. It is a Oneness that we see in so many of our age, Mother Teresa, Billy Graham, and Richard Foster.

It is Oneness that we all are invited to by Jesus. Come and Follow. Come and be with Me, come and live a life in Me. Come and experience what My Father first wanted in the Garden - Oneness.

We are tempted to read all these stories in the Bible and put them to the side. We are tempted to say we cannot be a Noah, we cannot be an Abraham, and we cannot be a Josiah or Hezekiah. It is beyond us to be an Abigail or Sarah or even an Elizabeth; and we would be correct. They had their own path; but, as each of their paths were to lead them to this ONENESS in God, so too is our path. While it will not look like theirs, it will have parallels, and it will be through the same power of the Holy Spirit that we all will share and live in. For it is not us in the end who creates this Oneness. It is the gift of Jesus. It is the gift of us laying down everything, sitting at His feet and opening up our hearts and lives to Him.

Yes, it will mean that we allow to fall away our own kingdoms, our own thoughts of personal power and position. But, once we obtain the ability to live and see in the Spirit, we will be able to look back and see how much rust and moth, how much sand those kingdom and possessions rested on.

Is it a call for everyone? Yes. Will everyone respond - that is an individual choice. Jesus is still calling those who will come and join Him. Those who, through His Holy Spirit, will allow the fire to fall, the winds to blow, and He will give you a whole new life - the life of Oneness.

Teach me to leave the
crowds of this world
Teach me to watch and
listen.

*Teach me to sit
in meadows
and fields
To receive and
feed on You.*

*Teach me to go to the kitchens of service
And to enter into a lifelong partnership with You.*

*Teach me to sit at your feet
And tune my heart to thee.*

Teach me to scale great mountains to behold your majesty.

*Teach me kneel beside
thee in gardens of
sorrow.*

*Teach me that in each
I behold your glory
and grow in my love
for thee.*

*Teach me to follow You only,
And put my future, myself, my everything in You.
For it will be only as I live in Your
Spirit that I shall find my life anew.*

SPIRITUAL DISCIPLINE #6
WORSHIP

In the year that King Uzziah died, I saw the LORD sitting high upon a throne, high and lifted up, and the train of his robe filled the temple. Isaiah 6:1 (ESV)

Make a joyful noise to the LORD, all the earth! Serve the LORD with gladness! Come before His presence with singing! - Psalms 100:1(ESV)

But the hour is coming, and is now here, when the true worshipers will worship the Father in spirit and truth, for the Father is seeking such people to worship him. God is spirit, and those who worship him must worship in spirit and truth. - John 4:23-24(ESV)

And when they had prayed, the place in which they were gathered together was shaken, and they were all filled with the Holy Spirit and continued to speak the word of God with boldness. - Acts 4:31(ESV)

Rejoice always, pray without ceasing, give thanks in all circumstances; for this is the will of God in Christ Jesus for you. Do not quench the Spirit. - 1 Thessalonians 5:9(ESV)

Then Jesus, calling out with a loud voice, said, 'Father, into your hands I commit my spirit!' - Luke 23:46a(ESV)

Worship is something that happens. It is experience. It is what Juliana of Norwich called being caught in God. "I saw Him, and sought Him; and I had Him, I wanted Him." Or, at least that is what can happen if we are open to worship the LORD.

Now, worship is something far different than what we call church time. The average US church attendee spends less than 60 hours a year in being a part of a "worship service". Now, what does that mean? The average person is awake about 112 hours (16 X 7) out of a week that includes some 168 hours. Of that 112 hours, usually 1.5 hours on average is dedicated to attending and being a part of a worship service. Which means, if we go to a service an average 60 hours a year, we are then spending approximately 1.03 % of yearly "awake" time in worship services. Now, when we look at worship in that regard, 1.03 % of our awake time, we fully understand that worship has to be more and include more than just our "church service time."

Worship is more than just our participating in the elements of what has been called worship - hymns, praise songs, Scripture readings, offering, preaching, Communion, and prayer. All of those can lead to a time of worship; but, the reality is we can participate in each of those activities and still not experience worship.

Worship is what happens when the glory of God falls down as it did in the Old Testament. It is when the Shekinah of God is ushered in or when we are ushered into the Shekinah of God. It is when the veil of heaven and earth is pulled back and we find ourselves understanding and experiencing the Presence of God. It is when we are surrounded by a mighty rushing wind, flames of fire and new understanding of language, and it is also when we are resting beside still waters and when we hear the whispers of God.

Richard Foster points us in the right direction when he says, "Worship is our responding to the overtures of love from the heart of the Father. Its central reality is found 'in spirit and truth.'" (*Celebration of Discipline*, page 138). There is no one form or ritual which produces worship.

Throughout history there have been many different forms and rituals. Robert E. Webber has edited a series of volumes that deal with all the different kinds of worship in a series called *Twenty Centuries of Christian Worship.* In reading those volumes, one is amazed at the different types and forms of worship that man has employed over the centuries.

Worship has been the experience of those who worshipped in home churches in the earliest days to those who filled the cathedrals of the mid 1500's. Worshipers have participated in the music of the Georgian chant to the music of Praise and Worship of today. Worship has been experienced by those who engage in purist of forms of the Latin liturgy to the avoidance of any kind of liturgy at all. In fact, what we find among all our people throughout the centuries is freedom. Freedom to worship God. For as one reads the New Testament, there is little evidence of a particular template for worship.

What we do find is individuals and congregations that did all they could to have Spirit touch spirit. What we find is that they would do whatever was necessary to prepare one's heart, mind and body to be in the Presence of Almighty God. It was to that end that was their heart's desire and the same is true today.

You can go all around the world and attend worship services that may not look the same, may not have the music, say the same prayers, or even take the Eucharist the same way but in each and every one of them there is one foundational and bedrock reality. Worship is always centered on God. Jesus answered for all time the question of Who we are to worship. *"You shall worship the LORD your God and Him only shall you serve"* (Matthew 4:10). To this there is no question, no discussion. True worship has been and always will be centered on God. He is the object of our worship.

Worship also has to be our first and foremost priority. If God is who He says He is, then worship must have priority in our lives. It cannot be something that we simply adhere to when it pleases us. Jesus tells us plainly, *"Love the LORD your God with all your heart, and with all your soul, and with all your mind, and with all your strength"* (Mark 12:30).

Now, given the fact that on average US evangelicals spend around 1% of their waking hours in "church worship," we can quickly see that on the surface we are not putting God first and foremost. I say on the surface because if we allow ourselves we can live lives of worship being in church and not being in church.

In the Early Church it was somewhat easier. For in the first few centuries one could gather for a time of worship daily. The Jewish model beforehand had been to participate in daily prayers three times a day and even more on the Sabbath. Naturally, the early church picked upon this idea and for centuries people participated in individual and corporate worship each and every day. Starting the day with morning prayers, continuing through the day with noon prayers, and ending the day with evening prayers. Added to these were Scripture readings that were to be read throughout the day.

Even now if one is a member of the Catholic, Lutheran or Presbyterian Church the use of a *Common Book of Prayer* is encouraged. Each day has a series of prayers and readings that are to be done to enable a person to prepare for corporate worship and to enable a person to experience worship each day of their life.

For again, worship is more than service. Worship is connecting with God. It is having your spirit connect with His Spirit. It is Adam and Eve's walk in the cool of the day. It is Psalm 23 being beside still waters. It is sitting at the feet of Rabbi Jesus. It is having the house shake after a time of prayer.

So, how can we best prepare ourselves for worship? If there is no certain template, what are we to do?

1. We are to prepare first and foremost by possessing a spirit of readiness, by believing first and foremost that God wants to be with us. Also, by adopting the same heart as Moses, and the Early Church, who

knew in their hearts, in the depths of their souls that God sought to be with them as much as they sought to be with Him. It is knowing that the GOD of all Creation desires to be with us, in us, and transform us.

2.	Second, we are to open our hearts. We are to open our hearts to be filled with the Spirit of God. Just as the Holy of Holies was dedicated to housing the very presence of God, so too, we open our hearts to experience God.

3.	It means that we close ourselves off to anything and everything that would hinder us. Even good things. We engage wholly. We engage body, mind, and soul. A great deal of the time this means getting some rest before our times of worship. It is difficult to worship on a Sunday morning if we have been playing out late on Saturday night. We wonder then why, with tired minds and exhausted bodies, we never experience worship on Sunday. If God is our priority it means that we come before Him ready physically, mentally, and spiritually to worship.

4.	It means we let go - we give all of ourselves to worship. We take a page out of King David's worship book and praise the LORD with all of our might. Our bodies were given to us to worship. We should be ready to stand, to clap, to lift up our hands, and even to dance before the LORD. To be smug, resist moving, and to wear a dour face is an affront to our God.

5.	It means that we wait, we become still and experience God. We must recapture Sabbath. Sabbath is 24 hours, not one hour a week.

We must understand if God is in control that pretty much means that He gets to show up when He wants to (remember that whole parable of the Bridegroom?). When we worship we are at His disposal, not the other way around. We are on His timetable and not ours. How many times have we missed an experience of God because we demanded that He be there from 10:30 to 12? Can you think of anything more arrogant? When we give God our whole Sabbath we open our lives to experiencing not only when we are at church, but throughout the whole day.

6. It means we become clay in the hands of God. We become focused, laser like focused on Him.

So many congregations have so much human centered activities in their worship time, activities that has very little to do with giving God praise and glory. Many times we get so caught up in all the human events and human activities that we fail to remember why we are there in the first place. It is not just to sing in the choir or to count the offering, acknowledge birthdays or anniversaries, or even to welcome one another. All of that comes out of a heart of service. Worship, although, is centered on God.

How many times have we heard someone say, "This is just not my type of worship," or "I desire a different type of worship." We all have different temperaments, and if worship was centered on us, then we could choose which ones we like and which ones we did not like. But the reality is, worship is suppose to be God centered. So, the question is not what do we like, but what kind of worship does God call for? What kind of worship experience is God looking for when we enter into His presence either as individuals or as a corporate body? It is clear that God seeks wholehearted worship.

The songs that we sing are not simply to be chosen by random. Hymns, songs, and musical specials are to be chosen to give Him praise. He is the focus of why and what we sing. While certain songs may be our favorites, we do God a disservice when we simply choose songs because we like to sing them or because they are our family favorites. Instead, we are to focus on what songs, what music, what things we can do to invite God's Presence into our times of fellowship. We sing songs to His glory, not to our ears. We sing songs to the Lover of our soul, not to the raising of our emotional needs.

Even our prayers are to be prayers focused more on thanksgiving and praise than they are to be simply prayers of intercession for healing and comfort. Yes, we are to intercede for the lost, for the sick, and for the needy; but, true worship is centered on Him. True worship includes the majority of our prayers focusing on giving God honor, praise, and glory. It is then that we are drawn to pray for one another and for ourselves. It is a matter of priority, and God must be first.

Whether worship is taking place in our home or at a building with other people present, the goal is for us experience worship. For that to occur it has to be God centered, with God having the highest priority in our hearts and lives. All too often we are tempted to be more concerned about taking care of one another's needs and before we know it, we have experienced a great time of human fellowship without experiencing any of God's presence or glory. It does not mean that we don't experience fellowship or take care of one another's needs. It simply means first and foremost the worship of God has to have ultimate priority. For when God is first, then lives, including our own, are transformed. We are changed. Dr. Jack Hayford is so correct when he states, "Worship changes the worshiper into the image of the One worshipped".

I remember years ago I found myself at a non-denominational service. Everything seemed to be going along quite nicely, nothing out of the ordinary. The music was uplifting the message was stirring, and then something happened that took me by surprise. It happened as we were preparing for Communion, the Lord's Supper.

I was raised in a tradition that focused more on the memorial aspect of the Lord's Supper than on being a present means of grace or a celebration. So, immediately upon hearing about the Lord's Supper, I went into a mode of confession and sorrow. Confession of sin and sorrow for the fact that our sins caused our Lord to have to die on a cross. For that is what I had been taught from the time of my childhood up. But suddenly, this young lady began singing this song of celebration and praise as they passed out the elements of communion. At first, inside my spirit I wanted to stand up and tell them to stop. They were not be reverent. How dare they sing songs of joy with communion. Everyone knew that communion was a time of great sorrow, a time of the burden of sin.

And then the Spirit asked me if I would like to worship. Would I allow Him to come in and teach me more about Him, to experience Him? Thankfully, I did not argue or grieve the Spirit. Instead, I allowed Him to come and the LORD's Supper took on a whole new meaning. Yes, our sins took Jesus to the Cross, but more than our sins, it was His love. For God so loved us that He sent His Son Jesus. Somewhere I had focused more on the sins, on the negative, than I had on the love. Love was and is the reason Jesus died and was raised again to forgive us of all our sins. Sure it was sin that caused our separation, but it was love that built the bridge.

Suddenly, what I had always had a difficulty seeing as worship, turned into this wonderful sacred moment of God's Presence and grace. Years later at Seminary when Dr. Staples encouraged us to view communion with the same joy, with the same spirit, with the same celebration as a group of hungry boy scouts around a campfire, I fully understood. Communion, the LORD's Supper became, and has remained, a vital moment of worship. It became a mean of being in His Presence. It became worship.

Years later kneeling at an Episcopal Church altar rail receiving a common cup so too came Christ. I had been raised with those nice little cups and those little tasteless pieces of square bread. Here I was invited to come and share in a common cup, an invitation to be one with Christ, in Christ, and to be one with the others at the altar. To share Eucharist, not as in individual, but as the corporate body of Christ. Worship happened. God came near.

That is what happens when we worship. Whether it is all alone as we read, meditate, and be quiet in His Presence. Whether it is in the mix of singing praise song, or liturgical hymns. Whether it is as we place our offerings into His hands, or when we listen to His Word, both read and explained. It may happen as we kneel in confession and prayer. But, it will happen if we are expecting, if we are open, if we put Him first and when all things are done to bring Him praise.

Worship can happen anywhere. It happened both at the pool of Siloam and at the synagogue. It can happen along the side of the road and it can happen inside a jail cell. It can happen whenever and where God is our focus and we dedicate body, mind, and soul to Him.

And when it happens, we are changed. If worship does not change us, it has not been worship. To stand before the Holy One and not be changed is to have not stood in front of the Holy One. We may have experienced a time of fellowship, even good fellowship, but we have not experienced worship.

Where there is worship, there is an increase in obedience and in love. It just happens that way. For to be in His Presence we join the Heavenly Host in making sure that in our lives His will is done. For that is the end of worship - obedience, increased love, and increased witness.

Worship propels us to say, Here am I, send me. Worship propels us to say, Not my will but Thy will be done. Worship propels us to think on things above, not on things below. Worship propels us to crucify the flesh and bear the fruit of the Spirit.

Where there are dissensions, where there are jealousies, where there are factions, there does not exist worship. Where there is worship, there is unity, there is Spirit and there is love, joy and peace.

Worship does not happen by accident. It happens when we come into the presence of the One we not only call Lord, but when we truly bow down and allow Him to be LORD of our lives.

"Many Spirit-filled authors have exhausted the thesaurus in order to describe God with the glory He deserves. His perfect holiness, by definition, assures us that our words can't contain Him. Isn't it a comfort to worship a God we cannot exaggerate?" ― Francis Chan, *Crazy Love: Overwhelmed by a Relentless God*

"I desire only Him and to be wholly His." - Brother Lawrence

Let us now worship Him!

EPILOGUE

There is so much more to share. This life of Oneness. This life of being all you can be in the Spirit. This life of experiencing God. While John and Mary both show us glimpses of what this life means, they are far from being the only ones. In their place we could have spoken about Abraham and Isaac, along with Elisha and Esther. Perhaps there needs to be another study done on the lives of the One. On the lives of those who have decided that they would pour out all of themselves in Christ, those who also belong to the Heroes of the Faith. Perhaps that is another study to be done at a later time.

Also, there are more than just these six spiritual disciplines. Along with those we need to practice the others like study, confession, giving, guidance, Sabbath and celebration; but, those too will have to be looked at in another context.

Hopefully, you have been intrigued. Hopefully, you have been challenged. Don't get comfortable in the crowd, or even the 5,000. Don't see being a part of the 72 as the highest point. God has invited us all to sit at His feet, all of us to follow Him, and more importantly all of us to be in Him. He wants to share life with us and in us. He has opened up His heart, if we will but accept His invitation to come and dine.

Living a life of Oneness is a lifelong journey. It is one that while it has a beginning, there is no end. There is no ceiling that can stop our progress and no floor that will deny our ability to grow deeper in the

LORD. There is only our desire that keeps us away from Him. We are as close to Him as we choose to be. Let us all choose to be ever more closer to Him.

APPENDIX A
Tabernacle Prayer

PRAYING THE TABERNACLE/TEMPLE PRAYER

Adapted from Pastor Cho for Griffin's Chapel COTN

Instructions: Pray the following pages out loud to learn how to worship God in the Tabernacle/Temple fashion. This prayer guide has been adapted from Pastor Cho of South Korea in a way to assist our times of prayer at the Griffin's Chapel Church of the Nazarene by Pastor Ernie L. Arnold.

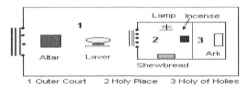

Opening Prayer:

Father we desire to pray today, so we come into Your presence right now – seeking only You! We cry out for Your anointing today! Anoint me, LORD JESUS! Only through more of Your anointing can I live out and carry out my work according to Your will for me. Only through more anointing can I fulfill Your plan for my life. Only through Your anointing can I live a victorious/sanctified life. Only through spending time in Your Presence Jesus can I ever hope to be completely filled with Your Holy Spirit.

Father, it was You who commanded Moses to build the tabernacle in the wilderness. You dwelt there and met Your people there. The Israelites worshipped only You in that tabernacle. They served no other god(s) in Your Tabernacle. It was holy and filled with Your Presence. The Tabernacle illustrates Your pattern for worship and for praise. It holds the sequence to draw close to You even today. I desire that intimacy today in my life. I desire to worship only You – Father, Son and Holy Spirit. I desire to be totally Yours – heart, mind and strength. I choose today to love You supremely!

I thank You for the tabernacle model through Moses, in Jesus, and in Heaven. I thank You for the courtyard – where the Brazen Altar and the Laver is located. I thank You for the HOLY PLACE – where the Golden Candlesticks are as well as the Table of Showbread and the Altar of Incense. I thank You for the HOLY OF HOLIES – where the Ark of the Covenant and Your Mercy Seat reside.

Today, according to Your Word – Your Spirit through the power of Jesus dwells within me. I am a clay vessel that can house both Your Holy Spirit along with my human spirit. My spirit can be in the Holy of Holies. My mind can be as the Holy Place. My physical body can be as the Courtyard. Come to me now, Lord Jesus! Work, cleanse, renew and revive my spirit. Flow through my spirit, my soul – my mind and body. I directly worship You, LORD JESUS, through the temple of my spirit, my soul, and with all my might. I turn myself over to You. Completely into Your hands I place myself.

Jesus, You are the High Priest of Heaven. Teach me Your Word, Your Way and Your Life.

Station One – THE BRAZEN ALTAR

In my imagination and in my spirit, I come to the Temple of the Holy Spirit. I see the Tabernacle Courtyard in my mind. I see the Brazen Altar. I remember all the different offerings that were presented on the Brazen Altar – SIN, TRESPASS, BURNT, THANKSGIVING AND RECONCILIATION. All of these simply foretold of the sacrifice of our LORD JESUS CHRIST. I acknowledge and recognize the cost of sin.

I believe the Cross of Jesus Christ, my Savior replaces the Brazen Altar for me today. I believe that the blood of Jesus replaces the blood of animals for me today. Jesus gave one sacrifice, Himself for all time. My sin is forgiven. I am declared righteous through the Cross of Jesus Christ. I have no guilt or shame today. I have been given and receive a clean slate today because of the blood of Jesus Christ. Thank You Jesus! I will enjoy forgiveness today. I will enjoy justification today. I will enjoy regeneration today. I will enjoy being Born Again today. I will enjoy living a life of salvation and sanctification. I will enjoy today being free from the penalty and

power of sin. I will today rejoice in living in Jesus Christ, my Savior and LORD!

Jesus, through Your shed blood conquered Sin. You defeated the Devil. You conquered Hell, death and the grave. I gratefully receive today Your sanctification and the fullness of Your Holy Spirit. Any hold that the devil or evil attempts to place on me is canceled and broken right now in the name of Jesus! Jesus today I acknowledge that You have delivered us from the power of darkness and in You we can experience a life of redemption and freedom. Because of the blood, because of Jesus, I am free in Jesus!

You hung on the cross for my infirmities. I am healed today. Sickness and disease are not to be mine. I will not claim a sickness or a disease, instead I call on the healing of Jesus in my life. By Your Stripes, Jesus we are healed. I claim Your healing today Jesus. I declare today in Jesus I am healthy in body, mind and spirit. I will not embrace any sickness or disease. Instead, I embrace Your Healing Jesus. I will bow at Your feet, walking with You always.

Through Your Cross – through Your Blood – I am redeemed. I am a new creation. You died on the Cross so that all the covenants shall be mine – the Adamic, the Noahic and the Abrahamic along with the New Covenant in Jesus. I am a blessed person! I am under Your blessing today, Jesus My Savior. I am under Your blessing as I go out and as I come in. Your face shines upon Me. Jehovah Jireh, You are my Provider. Jehovah Rapha, You are my healer. Jehovah Nissi, You are my Banner!

Jesus, You became poor so that I can be rich. Help me to seek Your Kingdom, Your righteousness, knowing that all my needs shall be meet according to Your riches in glory. In You, Jesus I am redeemed completely from any negative thinking. No cloudy thinking for me today – only clarity of my freedom from the curse and freedom from poverty.

I am redeemed from death, Hell and the grave. Through Jesus death on the cross, his resurrection and ascension I am redeemed today. His redeeming grace flows inside of my heart and life. Praise Jesus!

Thank You Jesus, that my mind is being renewed in when I pray this way. When I claim the truths and worship You. Thank You for renewing my spirit and mind that was clogged with lies and negative thoughts. I want nothing to do with the filthy things of this world. I reject all lies. I abhor all evil. I cut off every tie with the devil, with demons and with evil, in the name of Jesus. I want nothing to do with sin and things of this world. I declare today that I only want Jesus, I seek only to live a holy life.

Father, clarify my vision of myself as a person who has been forgiven, New Born and adopted into the family of GOD. Make me fully aware of my new identity – a redeemed, justified and regenerated person. A person who has been sanctified and continually being sanctified by Jesus Christ.   I have a clear identity in living in Jesus Christ.

I will not listen to the Devil today – I will not sign for any of his packages of lies.   I AM A NEW CREATION. I AM HOLY IN JESUS NAME! I AM SANCTIFIED! I AM BLESSED! I AM IN GOD'S FAVOR!

Station #2 – THE LAVER

FATHER, I INVITE YOU TO EXPOSE ANY SIN IN MY LIFE

It is here at the Laver that we cleanse our consciences, our lives every day like taking a bath or shower. It is here that we say again – Father forgive my trespasses. As the priests wash their hands, their feet at the Laver – so too LORD we ask that You wash us. As the priests used the laver as a looking glass – so too, LORD we ask that through Your , You help us see who we are today and who we can be today and tomorrow.   As I pray I reflect on Your Commandments to help me cleanse myself today:

I desire more than anything a holy relationship with You, Father! I desire Your way and Your will in my life.   I openly confess to You today, Lord that I need Your cleansing every day of my life. While I enjoy the fruit and experience of full blessing holiness, I also confess that I need Your sweet Holy Spirit to examine me each day. I confess to You today Holy Spirit I cannot live out a life of Entire Sanctification without You. And so, I bow before You to be examined by You and too, if need be, to confess my faults and to come under Your discipline, direction and renewal.

(It would be good for you to turn to Exodus chapter 20 and to simply go through each of the commandments and allow the Holy Spirit to use them as a renewal, discipline, and anointing tool)

Commandment # 1 – Holy Spirit am I worshipping any other gods? Do I put myself (self worship) ahead of Jesus? I know and acknowledge today that there is only one God, in three persons – Father, Son and Holy Spirit.

Forgive me, LORD for dishonoring You by entertaining other gods. I proclaim today that I love You LORD with all my heart, my soul, and my might. I proclaim that in my life there is only one GOD – YOU, LORD GOD ALMIGHTY!

Commandment #2 – Do I bow down to any idols? Have I placed my role as spouse, parent, and career person ahead of my role as a disciple of Jesus? Am I giving the first fruits of my day to something else? Am I worshipping the graven images of money or power?

Lord, forgive me for dishonoring You by worshipping any idols of any kind. Expose any false idols in my life. I reject anything that would come between me and You, O LORD.

Commandment #3 – Do I call Your Name in Vain – any of Your Names? Forgive me LORD by dishonoring You, by taking any of Your Names in vain. Help me this day to honor Your name, to honor Your presence and to glorify You in all my speech.

Commandment #4 – Do I honor You, LORD by keeping Your Sabbath HOLY? Forgive me LORD for dishonoring Your Sabbath commandment. Teach me Your ways, lead me in Your truths! Assist me, Father, in learning balance in my life. Help me to commit to a complete day of Sabbath rest. Help me to understand that in doing so I live out a life of balance, a life of trust, a life of being only dependent upon You.

Father as I do live out Sabbath – restore my mind, my body and my soul. Allow me Your rest, Your healing and Your grace.

Commandment #5 – Do I honor my parents or blame my parents for my problems? Do I dishonor those You have put in authority over me – my parents, my pastors, my bosses etc…? Do I gossip about them? Do I hold any grudges or hold any past sins against them?

Father, forgive me for the negative influence of the culture around me that disrespects our parents and dishonors You. May I be free of that evil influence in my life. Forgive me for dishonoring my parents and any that You have placed in authority over me. Thank You for my parents and for those over me. May You bless them and give them favor this day! May You help me to live in a way that I honor those

You have placed over me, praying for them and supporting them with words of encouragement and lives of obedience.

Commandment # 6 – Do I kill by hating? Father, show me if I have any malice or hatred for anyone at all. Show me if I have any grudges or anger today.

Father, in the name of Jesus today I forgive all others. I release all offenses and trespasses. I repent of any grudges or angry words spoken. Forgive me for dishonoring You through angry words and through acts of hatred. O Lord, deliver me from any bitterness. Only You, Jesus, can do this work in my heart. Only You, Jesus, can give me victory and grace in this area of my life. Thank You Jesus for Your grace, mercy and love. Thank You Jesus for victory.

Commandment #7 – Do I commit adultery or entertain lustful and impure thoughts? Forgive me, O LORD, if I have dishonored You by being sexually impure in thought or action. Cleanse my heart and my eyes. Cleanse me and make me holy! Give me the fear of the LORD. For the fear of the LORD is the beginning of wisdom, and the knowledge of the Holy One is understanding. Help me to walk softly before You – blameless. Deliver me from the idolatry of the human form. Allow me to see that Your creation is both holy and beautiful.

Lead me to walk in Your Spirit and not in the flesh. Lead me to walk a life of holiness in this important area of human life. Place a hedge of protection around me at all times. Clothe me with the armor of righteousness. Grant me Your wisdom, bind Your words on the tablet of my heart. Deliver me from unhealthy appetites, especially lust, which gives birth to sin and leads to death. Purify my mind, my heart and my life!

Commandment # 8 – Father, am I stealing from anyone? Am I stealing from You?   Father, show me if I am squandering or misusing Your Gifts that You have graciously given me. Show me if I am dishonest at work, taking anything without paying for it or asking permission. Forgive me O LORD for poor stewardship, for stealing or squandering time, talents and treasures from You. Forgive me for any dishonest gain and give me grace to return and restore what I have taken wrongly. Lead me into a life of honest stewardship of my time, my talents, and my resources. Help me to use that which You have placed in my care to bring honor and glory to Your name. Allow me to live out a life in which, in the end, I can hear the words – WELL DONE, THOU GOOD AND FAITHFUL SERVANT. Allow me to know a life of supernatural increase as I place everything in Your hands. Allow me the joy of being able to be a blessing to others in this life.

Commandment #9 – Father, am I being a truthful person?   Forgive me O LORD if there is any lying from my mouth. Forgive me for being a false witness of Jesus in my actions and in my words. Forgive me for believing any false ideas or vain philosophies. Father, my heart's desire is to be a true witness for Jesus. Sanctify my tongue, I place it today under the control of the HOLY SPIRIT. I cannot control this tongue of mine without Your Holy Spirit. Allow my words to only be a means of bringing forth a spring of fresh living water and the fire of Your Holy Spirit. I must speak, but let it be speech seasoned with the salt of Your Holy Spirit. Lead me in the way, the truth and the life in Jesus' name.

Commandment # 10 – Reveal to me Lord if I am coveting. Father, reveal to me this day if I am coveting anything that I do not have – my neighbor's house, car, reputation, wife, children or lifestyle. Forgive me, Lord, if I am coveting anything. I live in a nation built on the sinful love for money and the philosophy of coveting. Father, You are Jehovah Jireh – You have promised that You will provide all that I need. Jesus, You told me to seek Your Kingdom and all the things that I will need You will provide. Holy Spirit, just as You sent the quail to the ancient Israelites, so too will You provide my needs. I rest today in Your care. I rest today knowing that I will receive Your abundance and blessings! Your will be done in my life! Whether I have much or little, I praise Your Holy Name. Help me to see that I can be content in all things – knowing that I am in Your care.

STATION #3 – THE HOLY PLACE

THE CANDLESTICKS –

THE HOLY SPIRIT

I now enter, LORD, in my imagination and spirit into the HOLY PLACE. There I see the candlesticks, symbolic of Your Holy Spirit. The 7 candlesticks remind me of Your Holy Spirit who brings WISDOM, UNDERSTANDING, COUNSEL, POWER, KNOWLEDGE, FEAR OF THE LORD, AND HOLINESS.

Holy Spirit, today I welcome You in deeper ways in my life. I open up all myself to receive You and to be led by You. Dear Holy Spirit, I passionately desire Your anointing. I desperately desire today Your Wisdom. Help me to solve all the situations, all the problems that will arise in my life this day. Help me to know that today I can lean on Your wisdom.

Holy Spirit, I need Your Understanding. I need desperately to understand the deep truths of You, O LORD! I need to understand Your truths so that I can live out those truths and so I can pass them on to my children and all those around me.

Holy Spirit, I need Your counsel. I cannot walk this life without Your Light and Guidance. In my own strength, I do not know how to walk – either to the right or to the left. I do not want to walk on the wide way, but the straightway, the narrow way. If it pleases You, Holy Spirit, grant me words of counsel, wisdom and understanding that I may help others. I open my mind today to be led by You, Holy Spirit.

Holy Spirit, I need Your might – Your power! I want to be used by You as a vessel that can bring healing and deliverance to others.

Grant me this ministry – to help others find wholeness and to be free of evil in their lives. Infill me with Your Power so that I too may co-partner with You Holy Spirit in leading people to freedom and a life in the Spirit. Grant me the privilege of being Jesus to others – to lead others to You, Jesus. To enable them to experience the life in You, Jesus.

Holy Spirit, I need Your Knowledge. I do not always understand what I read in Your Word. I need You, Holy Spirit to open up my eyes and my mind to understand Your Word. Grant to me a keen fear of the LORD so that I will walk blameless before You. Grant me this so that I will walk softly before You and not commit any wrongdoing in my life. Sanctify me wholly through Your Word. Less of me, more of You, Holy Spirit! Again, Lord I confess my ignorance, my lack of intellectual ability but I know in You, Lord, there is knowledge, there is wisdom and understanding.

Holy Spirit, help me to live and understand that You are not a genie or an impersonal being. I acknowledge and worship You – You are Omnipotent, You are Omniscient, You are Omnipresent. You will anoint, baptize, guide, empower, and sanctify. You will guide me and be my comforter in this life.   I ask today for Your fruit to be made real in my life. Today, Holy Spirit I pray for You to fill me with love, joy, peace, patience, kindness, goodness, faithfulness, gentleness and self control. Holy Spirit, You are my senior partner, You are my LORD. I depend on You, Holy Spirit. Led me! Thank You Holy Spirit for Your anointing, for Your leading, for Your cleansing! I declare today I am following You and that I will follow You! I receive You, Holy Spirit. I rejoice in You, Holy Spirit!

STATION #4 – The Table of Showbread – SYMBOL OF HIS WORD

Thank You, Father for the WORD! Thank You for Your inspired Word. Thank You today for both Your Word and Your specific WORD for me today! Thank-You for my daily bread in Your Word.

Thank You Father for all of Your Word. Today I need Your WORD for my life. I need Your WORD to become more than just words on a page, I need to be able to digest them with my mind, my soul and spirit. So, I wait on You, Father. I want more than mere knowledge – for knowledge is fleeting. I do not want a "name it, claim it" relationship. I wait today Father for You to give Your WORD for me today! Lead me in Your Word. Teach Me in Your Word. Open up Your Word to me. Allow me to be a lover of the WORD. Place within me Your Word – truly allow me to have Your Word as my light and lamp as I walk this walk of Holiness. Help me to memorize Your Word – make it more than just words, but a part of my inner being. Fill my mind with Your Word. Place on my lips Your Word. Saturate My soul with Your Word. Reveal to me Your thoughts and teachings O LORD. Increase my faith – let me understand that faith comes by hearing and hearing by Your WORD. Jesus, You told us that we cannot live by bread alone – but instead we need Your WORD – make Your Word real in My Life today!

(Take some time right now and get into the WORD – whether it is a chapter or chapters or just a passage or even a single verse – allow the LORD to make His Word alive and real today in Your Life – this will take time – but, take it anyway – mediate on the WORD – don't leave until the HOLY SPIRIT is able to reveal to you what He wants you to have this day).

STATION # 5 – THE ALTAR OF INCENSE – SYMBOL OF THANKSGIVING AND PRAISE

Father, You are OMNIPOTENT – YOU ARE EL SHADDAI – ALL POWERFUL! You can do all things! Give me a perfect faith in You LORD JESUS!

I choose today free grace! I choose to believe in You! I reject fear and doubt. I reject the Devil and evil. I choose today to be positive and uplifting. I choose today to be a person of Praise and Thanksgiving.

I trust YOU LORD! I trust YOUR WORD, YOUR SPIRIT, YOUR HOLINESS! You are always with me. You will never leave me or forsake me.

And now LORD, I offer up prayers of incense (offerings of praise and thanksgiving) – I spend time praising You in my spirit. I ask for the help of the HOLY SPIRIT as I Praise YOU!!!

(NOTE: TAKE TIME TO JUST REST IN THE LORD. TAKE TIME TO JUST SIT IN PRAISE. JUST LET YOUR LIFE BE A SWEET INCENSE TO THE LORD – I would encourage you to take the time to just write down a few praises to the LORD. Allow the HOLY SPIRIT to lead you in a time of praise – sometimes you will be led to sing a song of praise. This is your time to just praise the LORD. (Don't skip this part or make it shallow – praising the LORD opens such new doors of anointing and blessing. It is through praise that much victory is won. It is through praise that our minds and souls are renewed, and it is through praise that we are transformed.)

STATION # 6 – THE HOLY OF HOLIES – THE ARK OF THE COVENANT

Thank You, Father for allowing me to come into Your Place – the Holy of Holies. I see the blood of Jesus sprinkled on the Mercy Seat. It is finished – Tatalistai. All my debts, all my sins have been paid for – I am free. I am free from the penalty and from the power of sin in my life. I am free from any bondage that the Devil tries to put on my life.

Through Jesus' blood I can become righteous. I am welcomed into the presence of God through the redemption of Jesus Christ. I praise You, Father, for the wonderful, incredible blessing of righteousness. I praise You, Father, for making me clean and inviting me into Your Presence to live forever and ever.

I am not clean of myself, I cannot earn it nor do I deserve it. However, Jesus, I receive from You today all that You want me to be – a sanctified whole person, one who no longer walks in the ways of the flesh, but is led and guided into the walk of the Spirit.

Jesus today I know You live within me and I within You, not as one who lives inside a house, not as a mere guest. But, as the One whom I have given control of my House, My Life – My Body, Mind and Soul. Jesus, You said we could be one with You – You prayed that we could be one with You as You are One with the Father and the HOLY SPIRIT We long for that Oneness! We declare today we are one with You – that we are one with the Father, Son and Holy Spirit.

We openly declare today that we are no longer of this world, even though for a time we must live in this world. We declare today that we are Yours, Lord Jesus. Jesus, make me one with You – with the Father – with the Spirit. Sanctify us in Your Truth. Make us a Holy People. We are HOLY! WE ARE ONE! WE ARE IN CHRIST!

Empower me to go into the world, to not be a part of the world, but to share Your Good News. Grant me the courage and boldness to speak Your Word. Grant me the ministries of healing and signs and wonders done in Your Name. Fill me again with Your Holy Spirit.

Make me one with others of faith – make us complete in You. Holy Spirit, lead us to a life in which we are kind to one another, in which we are fervent in spirit, and in which we are rejoicing in hope. Jesus, help us to love one another today.

And now LORD as in my mind, I kneel beside Your Mercy Seat – the Ark of the Covenant, I pray the prayer of the Great Commission. I pray for those closest to me (family, friends). I pray for those around me (my community) and I pray for others (the world).

(TAKE TIME NOW TO BRING YOUR REQUESTS TO THE LORD - PRAYING FOR YOUR FAMILY, YOUR FRIENDS, FOR THE LOST AND

UNCHURCHED. FOR NEW MINISTRIES, FOR YOUR CHURCH. FOR YOUR ENEMIES. FOR THOSE WHO HURT YOU. FOR ALL OTHER THINGS THE LORD PLACES ON YOUR HEART).

End your time today in thanksgiving and praise. Thank the LORD for answered prayer and for His Presence. Thank the LORD for sending answers, changing lives, and moving mountains even right now. Thank the LORD for all things. Rejoice in Him.

Made in the USA
Monee, IL
11 November 2020